MW01075054

CALLED TO THE MIDDLE

Copyright © 2016 by Joseph E. Eidson

All rights reserved. No part of this book may be used or reproduced in any manner whatsoever without written permission except in the case of brief quotations embodied in critical articles or reviews.

www.joeyeidson.com
www.calledtothemiddle.com

Cover Design by Brandon Hix
Edited by Keri Bostwick

For Us By Us

ISBN: 978-0-9975520-1-0

First Edition: July 2016
Printed in the United States of America

Table of Contents

INTRODUCTION

One of the common myths of education is that middle school educators really want to be with older students and are just settling for middle school until something better comes along. Another myth in education is that middle school students are just smaller and smellier high school students. Just like almost every other middle school educator I know, I set out to teach a different age group and found myself in middle school. Middle school is without question the most difficult age group to educate. They are not high school students, and they are no longer elementary students. They are middle school students, and they are experiencing difficulty in their lives on several fronts: physically, emotionally, socially, and academically. There is a special group of people who understand and enjoy middle school students. Some of us who teach middle school wonder if we are in purgatory on earth or if we have the best job in the world. One thing is certain: every child deserves the opportunity to attend a middle school with teachers who love their job, classrooms that are engaging and geared for their age group, and a school that has a welcoming environment for them to grow and mature into the young adults they will soon be. This book is dedicated to those special individuals who have answered the call and teach in the middle.

PART ONE

THE EFFECTIVE TEACHER

ONE

THE CALL

"I dream of growing up and teaching seventh grade math", said no child in history. Few people ever plan to teach middle school. Most people get hives at the thought of immersing their life with a day full of adolescents. Children and adults know the unique characteristics of a thirteen-year-old. Most people shake their heads when a middle school employee answers the question of occupation. It is almost like they heard you had some incurable disease. They act as if it is a penance that must be paid. We must have done something wrong in our former life. Teaching middle school could possibly even be an act of self-punishment. Some people will even thank me, basically saying someone has to do it.

I recently took a trip to a middle school conference. On a bus ride downtown I sat next to a lady with a walker who struck up a conversation very quickly by asking me if I knew the definition of reverse osmosis. I looked up the Wikipedia definition on my phone, leaned over toward her so she could read it and she screamed, "Well, read it to me" in a very raspy voice (My colleague was just grinning at me). I consistently attract the strangest situations. She scooted closer to me as I read the definition. Then she asked me to read the definition of osmosis. I read the definition to her and she explained her theory of why she had been sick, despite what the doctors had told her. I couldn't quite understand where this conversation could be going, but after about five minutes the conversation took a turn when she asked me what I did for a living. I told her I was a principal. She said, "At a high school?" I said "no, a middle school." She yelled at the top of her lungs, "Why? They're like bats out of hell! I taught school for thirty years and we all decided if you're a bad person in this life you'll have to teach seventh grade for eternity. Why do you do that? Do you like it there?" she asked. I told her that I like middle school. She looked at me with great confusion. I looked at the faces of several other passengers and saw grinning and snickering all the way back. Unfortunately, I think most of them agreed with her. She then asked my colleague, another middle school principal, the same set of questions. She shook her head and mumbled the same thing over about why would anyone want to teach in a middle school, those kids are crazy.

When I think of my career in middle school, I know that I have enjoyed making a difference every day. I had a terrible middle school experience as a child, but the opposite can be said for the students in my school. The mass majority of alumni come back and talk about middle school being the best experience despite their awkward disposition. We learn, we laugh, and we play every day. At our building, we enjoy making a difference in our students and we do not let anyone fall through the cracks. It takes an entire building full of likeminded educators to make this possible.

There is indeed something special about a group of professionals who choose to spend their days investing in these students. They not only spend their time investing, they are responsible for student performance on state exams. They make a choice to work in a middle school because they feel that is the age group they are called to teach. They walk through the doors of a middle school every day like a soldier entering the battlefield. These are the most difficult students to handle. They can sense weakness of any kind. They don't automatically go to their seats like a high school student. They don't come tell you when something is wrong like an elementary student. One mistake will cost you. You have to be well prepared to step on to that school property every day. Middle school teachers do not take the day off, hardly even when sick, because they know what can happen when they are gone.

Just like a scene out of _A Few Good Men_ where Jack Nicholson says, "You want me on that wall. You need me on that wall!" We do want those middle school teachers in that classroom. We need those middle school teachers in their classroom. This is what they are called to do in life. What would we do with those students all day if we didn't have competent classroom teachers? I imagine terrible anarchy where the entire world falls apart. We need the best, brightest, most patient teachers in the world filling our middle school classrooms. We would not want there to be questionable people in our military or our emergency personnel. We need the best people to watch over us and protect us. We also need the best people to invest and watch over our students.

When I am talking about a middle school educator, I am speaking of those unique individuals who have found themselves in the middle and love what they get to do every day. Those special people who relate to middle school students and seek to help them transition from a child to an adult with the least amount of turbulence. They work with a team of individuals with a shared mission to put student interests first. Every scheduling decision, every meeting, and every lesson plan is about what is best for students. Student connections, relationship cultivation, and academic success are the order of every day. Nothing short of miracles in behaviors and academic advancements will satisfy a middle school educator. They have energy that is unexplained. They have skin that is thick, because even good students will pick a middle school teacher apart. Adolescents can be the world's greatest critics. A teacher at this level can tell you everything wrong with them because it has been pointed out many times over. Middle school teachers shake it off and move along, a quality that very few people possess. They are also very soft and comforting when those same students let down their guard and need someone to speak about their problems. So, where do these teachers come from?

I am sure those who read this book won't be surprised to find that people are not lined up out of college to teach in middle schools. Teachers come to job fairs with either an elementary or a secondary degree. Middle school is an afterthought until prospective teachers realize they may not get their dream job in an elementary or high school. A few colleges are just now beginning to offer middle level education degrees, but I have yet to see one on a resume. Great middle schools have principals who are recruiters. They find quality elementary or secondary teachers and recruit to the middle level.

I entered a classroom one day to check on a class. The teacher had asked the administrators to check on her last two classes because they were on the brink of being out of control. We took turns and made daily visits. When I opened the door, a young lady who had the appearance of a high school student looked at me and asked if I needed anything. I stated that I was just checking on the class. She turned around, commanded the student's attention, and started the lesson. The students were somewhere between shock and appreciation for structure. I was amazed that this substitute could assert that level of calmness to a class that was anything but calm on a daily basis. Several months later I saw that substitute at a job fair and requested that she come to my table for an interview. I knew she needed to be a middle school teacher. She has been teaching seventh grade for four years and she is an amazing instructor.

Teachers learn very quickly their niche and middle school is not for everyone. As a matter of fact, very few educators can handle a middle school classroom. I have seen the frustration level come over teachers who think they are up for any challenge. Very intelligent, wonderful people with pure intentions and creative lessons have been taken to a personal and professional low by a room full of early adolescents. In all branches of the military, there are groups they identify as Special Forces. These groups take on more training and have intangibles that make them stand out. Rest assured that effective middle schools have a group of teachers who would qualify as Special Forces in education. Only a handful of well-trained professionals can safely engage thirty middle school students.

As an administrator, finding the right person for each position in middle school has been a great challenge and blessing. People usually apply for 7-8th grade positions if they cannot find the right high school position. Elementary teachers can be interested in sixth grade positions if the upper elementary positions are not available. Certifications then become an issue because they have to be highly qualified. A principal might spend a significant amount of time on the phone with the state department to make sure an applicant is highly qualified to teach at the middle level. If you find the right person for middle school, you cannot let them go. Sometimes teachers have to take extra tests. The main goal is to find the right teacher to engage a middle school classroom. Middle schools need teachers who belong in the middle. Students need teachers who belong in the middle.

In a survey of fifty certified educators in a thriving, highly effective middle school, only two teachers had planned to teach middle school. I would guess that if you gave the same survey to a high school or elementary school, you would probably see opposite results. This middle school is Madison Middle School, and we believe in the middle school concept. I believe we are all the adjectives above because we love middle school; we choose to be here; we know what we want our students to learn; we connect to every student, and we make sure our students thrive. We are constantly getting better at reaching our students. Most of our former students will attest that their middle school experience was great. We work with likeminded educators to make middle school a positive experience, just like many other middle schools across the United States. I could give the survey to hundreds of other schools and teachers, but I know the results would be similar. Very few plan to teach in middle school because it is a forgotten age.

Most people attempt to forget that time of their life. When their children get to that age, many times they want to forget they had children. Their children do not want to be seen with their parents at this point either. They are not the cute elementary kids that crawl in your lap to read a book when they get home. They aren't the cool high school student you envision becoming an adult very soon and hope to be friends with someday. They are middle school kids. They are smelly, moody, and exhausting. At some point in middle school, parents lose hope their child will ever grow out of this stage. Society wants to ignore this age. It is so important that we do not allow them to be invisible. It is important that we prepare for these adolescents.

We have to embrace this age group. They need us to embrace this age group. Middle school students are making life decisions every day. They are deciding what kind of person they are going to become by watching others. They are learning how to treat their peers and adults by the examples they see daily. They are monitoring everyone around them to figure out where they belong and what is appropriate. We need the best group of trained individuals, who have the desire to work with this age in the classroom, fully equipped and supported.

Most of the individuals surveyed found themselves in the middle, including myself. Some people planned to teach high school. Some planned for lower elementary. Many planned for upper elementary. Some people found a favorable schedule for coaching and this was an open position. About half of the teachers had worked in an elementary or high school before. One thing is for certain, all of them want to be in the middle and appreciate the opportunity to affect lives every day. They have realized their potential in the academic and personal lives of the individuals they get to teach. They understand that there are not many people who can handle what they do on a daily basis and they wear that badge proudly. They are excited when school starts. Breaks from school are great, but these teachers don't view their positions as jobs; these positions are a life fulfillment. They prefer working with students rather than meeting with a group of adults all day.

Asking one of these middle school teachers if they are just waiting for a high school position is offensive to most of them. Many can teach high school, but minimizing their impact on the lives of students for a group that is more popular is insulting because they fulfill a role that few could ever handle. It is much more than just a job or a current position, these teachers are on a team and a mission together. Their success means lives have been altered and paths have been straightened. Students have been given every known opportunity to be successful. Most parents will never know how fortunate they are to have teachers who fill their children's life daily with positive role models.

There is no doubt a call on the lives of people in different services and occupations. Sometimes people have a job that they do for money and a call on their life for other purposes. My friend Dennis has a managerial job in retail, but his passion is the guitar and he is incredibly talented. He plays for his church every Sunday and gains great fulfillment by leading worship. I have other friends who volunteer in missions and food kitchens because they get gratification out of helping others. I know people who have been affected by disease and their call is to raise awareness and support for their cause. I have several friends who are called to full time ministry. There are dozens of people who mentor youth through Run The Streets in Bartlesville, while working full time in other professions. RTS is a program where mentors spend countless hours running and encouraging students to accomplish a half-marathon. Many students have been in trouble with the law and this is their one way out. What a wonderful way to help improve the lives of children. When people fulfill the calling on their lives, they approach it with passion and fervor.

If you are a middle school teacher and you enjoy your time in the classroom, there is not a doubt that you have a call on your life. It isn't for the money. There aren't any teachers choosing education for the paycheck. Teacher pay is not ideal in any state, particularly the state where I reside. Going to college is tough enough, but attaining certification and keeping it current is tedious. Most teachers could significantly increase their income in the private sector, but they understand their fulfillment doesn't come from a paycheck; it is people – particularly adolescents- who motivate and move them.

Those called to the middle feel a need to contribute to the lives of students. They take their passion for their content and pour themselves into creative lessons that will light a fire under their students. They are creative and committed. When a student understands a new concept or takes an interest in the subject, the middle school teacher enjoys the success of the moment. That short pause only fuels their fire to create more. Middle school teachers work furiously to get to know their students so they can pique their interests and get them excited about percentages or pronouns. In middle school, lessons are written with specific students in mind; nothing happens by accident. Teachers target specific students with each lesson in the hopes that during that lesson, someone will be moved.

They don't work this hard for the money, and they don't work this hard for the gratitude. Sometimes students thank a teacher. Sometimes their parents thank a teacher and let them know how much they appreciate the effort to invest in their child. These teachers work this hard because they know they changed a life. They changed the world. They infused the shy reader with confidence and the frustrated teenager with self-esteem. Many people can recall that one teacher who changed their life.

I had a terrible experience in eighth grade art. The teacher wouldn't let us talk and I sat next to my best friend. Many after school detentions were bestowed upon me that school year, which meant that I had to report to the janitor for free labor. Currently, I have the wonderful opportunity to work with an art teacher who desires for her students to explore and understand art. She devises opportunities for her students to be creative and display their works of art. She integrates art with physics, math and history. Sometimes there is music playing in the background and the students move around freely working on projects. They openly communicate and enjoy the learning environment. The first time I observed Julie teach, I told her I wished I could have had her for art when I was in eighth grade. After observing Julie for a couple of years, I discovered that she is a highly intelligent, very balanced individual who had a multitude of opportunities with her skillset. She chose to teach because she felt a call on her life. She has the opportunity to facilitate students discovering the artist inside of them, which is scary for most of them. She shows them how to express themselves through art.

A good school should help every person in it – the teacher, the principal, the janitor, the student – to discover who she or he is. Some of this is intentional by teachers; more happens by walking through the fire that is middle school. When a teacher walks in to the classroom for the first time, her students size her up. The first time that teacher steps up to the podium, he is being scrutinized with every squeak of his shoe. Call it curiosity; call it cruelty. Whatever you call it, it is a truth middle school teachers know intimately. And they welcome it. They embrace who they are and are not defined by anyone else's definition of them. Effective middle schools help teachers know who they are and why they are there.

Not only do they know themselves, but teachers who are called to the profession know their students. This doesn't happen by accident; it is an intentional aspect of each lesson for the middle school teacher. They know what their students' interests are; they know who their crushes are. They know what causes them pain at home and in the hallway. It is part of the reward and burden of teaching. The smallest successes are a celebration and the tribulations of this age are dramatic. Middle school teachers think they have heard it all, until the next day.

Most teachers know it is a privilege to get up every day and go to school. They get the opportunity to invest in students. Unlike a job "in the real world", where money is the name of the game, education is investing in lives. Education is about people, little people who will grow up right before our eyes. They may become productive members of society or a burden on society. They may grow up to hate art or love art. Teachers know it is their responsibility to make sure a student learns the objectives for each class. They embrace the opportunity to instruct. Teachers who are called to education know they have the best job in the world. They have found their place in this world. It is both exhausting and fulfilling.

When exploring the road to investing in the lives of middle school students, the map gets muddled. What works one day could fail the next. You could have a distraction at any moment. There might be an assembly, fire drill, girl drama or a full moon. It is an obstacle course every day of every school year. These early adolescents are the most unpredictable creatures on the face of the earth, similar to the weather in Oklahoma. Middle school teachers know how to punt. They know how to change a lesson midstream or condense a lesson in a time crunch. One thing is for certain, you will never be bored in middle school. If you are still reading, you might be a middle level teacher.

Do you enjoy active lessons where you get to facilitate student learning (This isn't lecture hall; middle school requires active learning)? Will your brain allow you to remember what it felt like walking in to middle school or junior high? Do you find yourself empathetic toward awkward individuals who are in between a child and adult? Do you enjoy every day being completely different? Do you still like to laugh and play games? Can you team with a group of professionals to seek the best interest of all students? Do you mind being idolized? You might be a middle school teacher.

The remainder of this book is in three sections: The middle school teacher, the middle school classroom, and the middle school structure. The next chapter will describe the middle school student by grade level and the special teachers who fulfill their call every day.

TWO

THE KIDS

The middle school student is fascinating. There is never a dull moment. We have all lived through early adolescence. Most people quickly and purposefully forget this special and malleable time of their life. You never know what will happen in the day of an early adolescent. It is truly miraculous to watch them grow so rapidly in such a short amount of time. Their time in the middle is quick but extremely important. Their brain is in overdrive all of the time. They live a lifetime of emotions in a year. They look back six months and feel as if that was a time when they were little and immature. They see a picture from a year ago and get embarrassed at how young they were. They are moody, fun, energetic, loyal, needy, dramatic, passionate, emotional, caring and kind. They are scary in groups and scared individually. The middle school student is constantly looking for acceptance.

Middle school students are the best if you can handle them and you can handle what they do to you. They arrive as children and leave young ladies and men, and it happens in a flash. Most of them nearly double in size during their three-year tenure. They have a ton of energy and they want to have fun. They can't fathom the idea they will be all grown up in a few short years, hopefully in college or contributing members of society. They love to laugh, but are truly insecure at all times. They value relationships with peers above all others. They also need positive and rational adults in their life. Middle school students need acceptance from everyone. They become so much more self-aware. They become aware of how they look and how much they weigh. They become aware of their socio-economic status. They become aware of the opposite sex. They become aware of their intelligence level. They can also become aware of their strengths and interests, if they are in an environment that cultivates the opportunity to explore their gifts.

The following chapter describes a middle school student by grade level and a description of their teachers and how they are able to instruct and reach these students in effective middle schools. Although they have many similarities as middle school students, each grade level is very different. Fifth grade is considered middle level in many schools, but it is not included in this chapter because my experience is in a traditional middle school with sixth thru eighth grades, the area in which I consider myself an expert. I have heard fifth grade students have very similar characteristics to sixth graders, and can be interchanged at times, but I am sure they have other characteristics that could be included by experts who work with them daily.

Sixth grade students arrive the first day of school awkward and fearful. No matter how many times we get to interact with these students before this monumental day, they get anxious the first day of school. We give tours of our building with their parents in the spring, where they get to take a scavenger hunt of the building, practice locker combinations and meet the teachers. We have each feeder elementary bring their 5th grade over during a school day, where we introduce them to all of our performing arts, clubs, and activities. We give them another tour of the building and let them eat lunch with the current sixth grade and experience the playground. We even offer a one-week transition camp during the summer. Transitions are the toughest obstacles for students, and we want the smoothest transition possible. We take every opportunity our elementary partners will afford us to let the incoming sixth grade students familiarize themselves with middle school. Many parents walk them to the door and even come in for a minute the first day of school. Students will immediately gravitate to familiar territory with their friends from elementary school. They are full of giggles and smiles. Most sixth grade students remain very concrete during those first months of school. They will believe almost anything you tell them with a straight face. Sixth grade students will blurt out any personal familial information without a blink, even information that can emotionally disturb the adult recipient. They are still silly and very moldable. They want to feel at home and safe. They need to be nurtured, loved, and protected during the transition from elementary to middle school. Every adult remembers the first day of Jr. High/Middle School. Those days can be exciting or traumatizing. It is important that this first semester is positive and adults control the environment.

Sixth grade students are hyper active. They need to get everyone's attention. Most students stay completely positive, even when going overboard with their behavior in class. They have spatial issues. They have a tendency to get in the teacher's bubble. They have to be told their boundaries. It isn't unusual for a sixth grader to walk up and hug their principal the first day of school. They are adorable and fragile those first days of school. They are excited and scared. They lose those adjectives after a couple of months. They need to be protected from older students but integrated enough to see what to expect. They need to be loved and cared for by all of their teachers. It isn't enough for them to make a connection with just one teacher. They are looking for acceptance. As they change during the year, they need to feel secure. They get awkward and go through multiple phases. As they begin to go through changes, so does their choice of friends. They get to know new friends from other elementary schools. They realize they have new interests and befriend others who have those same interests. It is a positive attribute and it takes them out of their comfort zone. They also start to consider themselves friends in large groups, particularly the girls.

One day as a teacher, I overheard a group of students reminiscing during micro-society. This was our last hour class on a Friday afternoon and they were supposed to be planning for the next week. Students were talking as if I was not in hearing distance. (If you don't make eye contact, a middle school student does not believe you are listening.) An 8th grade student who I had in class, coached and had known her family for several years stated, "I didn't know anything until sixth grade, then I learned everything." Her face dictated she was a bit traumatized by the amount of information she received, and it was all on the bus. She was talking about sex. She saw me look up, and we caught eyes. I had watched her grow up and I remember when she came to the school. I was absolutely appalled. She was just an innocent tiny little girl in sixth grade. She didn't weigh fifty pounds. I couldn't imagine that she would get that kind of information. I looked at her and said, "Are you serious?" At that point a group of students made me aware that sixth grade is the year they learn about sex. If they haven't been educated by their parents, they will learn about it from their peers. Through many conversations with parents and students as an administrator, I have confirmed that as a fact. They will learn all about sex in sixth grade.

Sixth graders start out elementary students but end the year full-blown middle school students. The transformation is subtle through the year but sudden when you pause to remember who they were just a few months prior. Their physical stature changes dramatically. Their emotional state changes from a little kid to an early adolescent.

Sixth grade teachers at both middle schools I have worked have done a phenomenal job integrating some elementary procedures and techniques to calm student nerves. An effective middle school 6th grade teaching team will plan activities and lessons that coincide with each core class to make those students feel very comfortable. A teacher to shake their hand, help them with their locker, walk through procedures and show a level of patience, calms the nerves, and the world suddenly brightens for an anxious little soul those first weeks of school. The old junior high theory that we will baptize students with new strict rules and make an example out of a few, so the rest will follow out of fear, traumatized the past generations. Students don't need anyone barking orders and blowing whistles to get their attention. Middle school students are not miniature high school students. Their brains are not developed and there is no sense in the "Shock and Awe, you're in my world now" approach.

Sixth grade students, who are cultivated in a caring environment in an effective middle school, will mature naturally throughout the year. They become much more independent in their abilities and their confidence gradually grows. At some point during their sixth grade year, they become early adolescents. It takes a special group of adults to create an atmosphere where students feel safe and secure in their learning environment. A sixth grade teacher is mom, dad, teacher, and counselor every day. The reward is incredible. Helping students grow and mature socially and academically is akin to a parent at school. The teachers at Madison talk about their students as if they were their personal children. It is their responsibility not only to teach them but make sure they are ready for all aspects of the next level of life. During a thumbs meeting (talking about students), sixth grade teachers can beam with joy over the last triumph or hold their head in frustration of what to do for a particular student because s/he seems to be slipping through the cracks. One thing is certain, the impact on that child's life is beyond measure and they need the right person in that classroom.

Seventh grade students come to enrollment two weeks before school starts, and they are ecstatic. They are perceptive enough to know they want to be on the same teaching team as their friends because they want to be in classes together. "Their friends" usually consist of a massive group. They will even have their parents request team changes to be with their friends. They are full-fledged adolescents. Most of them have grown several inches, and they are confident in their abilities to navigate the middle school. If they haven't already hit puberty, they will very soon. Physical changes are inevitable and they don't want attention drawn to them. The girls are trying to get the boys' attention, and the boys are typically oblivious. Boys are concerned with football, basketball, soccer, video games or some other adrenaline related activity. Even when they like the girls, very few can carry on a conversation with the girl he is obsessing over.

In seventh grade, students are usually laughing on the outside and extremely insecure on the inside. Even the "pretty girls" or the "cool guys" are insecure. When middle school students are asked which year was the toughest during their tenure, most have said seventh grade. They are so confused and have no idea why emotions are changing on a dime. Seventh grade students' eyes break loose and begin to roll whenever an adult is talking. Even great students will accidentally roll their eyes when they do not highly favor your answer to their question. It is hard to find any true leadership in seventh grade because all the students want to blend in with the crowd. They are an extremely playful group who love to be active all of the time. Seventh grade students need a distraction from themselves. They need to be so busy with positive activities inside and outside the classroom that they are distracted from the changes going on in their bodies and minds.

Seventh graders are unpredictable. If a child is going to have a meltdown, it is likely to be in seventh grade. If a child is going to have a sudden drop in their grades, it will happen in seventh grade. If they are going to have an emotional collapse, this is their year. They could be hyperactive-happy or a crying, emotional mess. They experience extremes and it affects everything. This could be due to the sudden influx of hormones in their bodies.

Although mood swings and meltdowns are concerning,

none of us would like to experience the activity happening within their bodies. Imagine having a shot of testosterone you didn't know was coming. It would be like taking drugs without your knowledge. They may be at football practice where they get to hit, tackle, run, and yell at the top of their lungs. They might be at wrestling where they get to take their energy out on the mats. They also might be in class where they get overwhelmed with a homework assignment they feel is impossible to complete with the activities they have later. They walk out frustrated and hit a locker. They might bump in to another charged young male and get in a fight before they even realize they are angry. A boy who has never been in trouble his entire life could get in a fight before he can think about the consequences. This happens more often in seventh grade than any other grade level.

A girl might have a complete meltdown because her friend isn't talking to her. Her boyfriend breaks up with her, and she cries for hours. It may be the same boy who broke up with her two months ago that was no big deal, but this time it is an emotional catastrophe. It is because she was naturally drugged with estrogen and she never saw it coming. This is the true age of drama for the girls. They still have not figured out that they cannot be best friends with seventy other girls. Seventh grade girls actually think they can make decisions in masses. They believe they can get large groups of girls to all agree. Drama will usually erupt in seventh grade, and counselors get the challenge of sorting it out. students have to be taught how to handle situations. Seventh grade student reactions are completely unpredictable, and they are unstable for good reason. It isn't anyone's fault; they need time to mature. These students need people who understand them. They need people who want to be around them. They need consistency in their lives. Some students have consistency at home; some do not. Everything about them has become inconsistent: their peers, their emotions, their ideas. They need consistency at school. They need teachers who give them stability through solid structure, a nurturing environment, and high expectations.

There is possibly no more of a noble cause than to work with seventh grade students. Seventh grade teachers at effective middle schools embrace the opportunity to challenge their students. They choose this age group. They want to teach students who are moody and self-conscious. They love students who are hyper active and needy. They are completely immune to the eye roll. They are prepared for the natural drug infusion. Madison Middle School teachers are excited to reach these students every day. They hug and high five these students all day. Their students love their teachers because they want to be in those classrooms. They know they have the skills to maintain an environment conducive to learning, and the reward is great.

The teachers at this grade level are excited about their students' academic and social growth. I have witnessed a phenomenon that I do not see in other grade level teachers. Seventh grade teachers are even more energetic *after they teach*. They walk out of the room excited about how their lesson unfolded and how the students reacted to the new activity. They get ecstatic when a student steps out of their comfort zone and begins to talk in front of the class. Often these teachers are giddy when the last bell rings. They are blessed with boundless energy.

Seventh grade students don't understand boundaries in relationship information. If they trust their teacher or counselor, they will share information about their feelings for the opposite sex. If you are a passerby or a new parent to seventh grade relationships, it can be a shocker to hear the blunt exchange of information.

Seventh grade teachers are sensitive to the hormone influx and student breakdowns. They know how to calm dramatic groups of girls and stabilize aggressive boys. Great teachers are not immune but prepared for these students. Students never forget those who love and protect them during the goofiest, most awkward stage of their development. It is common place at Madison to see students go straight back to their seventh grade teachers to say hello, get advice, or just sit back and have a conversation. High school students come back to see their seventh grade teachers. Anyone who had a meaningful seventh grade teacher in life, one who cared about you and protected you, owes them a thank you.

Eighth grade students know it all, just ask their parents. They are definitely excited to be the oldest. At an effective middle school, these students understand they are the leaders of the school. It is their responsibility to lead in a positive way. They need to be given ample responsibility and opportunity to prove they own their school. NJHS and Student Council should be loaded with eighth grade students. When the leadership of eighth grade is strong, it effects the entire culture of the class and even the school. Eighth grade students take pride in mentoring sixth and seventh graders at an effective middle school.

This is typically their best year in middle school. They understand themselves a little bit better. They are confident. They walk down the hallways with swag. The trials and tribulations of seventh grade are just a spot in the rear view mirror if they've had effective teachers. They are much more comfortable in their own skin. They still have all the hormones and they still have all of the issues, but it is no longer new to them. They can look back and appreciate they have reached a new level.

Eighth grade students are living in the moment. They literally want to have a great time every day. They usually aren't thinking about high school until late in the spring. Most of them have not figured out the dynamics of high school or what their future looks like. They are not looking back; they are not anticipating the future. They are more mature with their energy, but it still abounds. They are much more abstract and can understand facetious humor. They can laugh at themselves. They have given up on trying to have a multitude of friends. They know they have a few close friends and the rest are just buddies. Generally speaking, there is much less drama in eighth grade for that reason. Girls have given up trying to make impossible decisions in the masses. Boys are much more aware of the girls and try to get their attention at any cost. Real couples and actual relationships emerge.

Students are calmer in the hallways but still need to be active in the classroom. In middle school, there is a level of self-control privy only to eighth grade. They understand when they control their behavior, they get more freedom. They have become more aware of their skillset. If they are talented at art, technology, athletics, or performing arts, they will want to hone in on that skill. They will hang out exclusively with other students of the same interest.

Eighth grade teachers keep positive things in front of their students at all times. Anytime they have an opportunity for a class simulation or active learning, teachers seize the chance. They know eighth grade students lead positively or negatively. Eighth grade classrooms at Madison are incredible. There isn't one class that you will enter without becoming a part of the learning experience. The teachers know these are the students they were called to teach. The journey begins each year with a wide-eyed group of students who are excited to experience all of the opportunities and activities they have seen the previous eighth grade students enjoy.

Eighth grade teachers know they are responsible for the leadership of the class. They take it personally when an administrator corrects the class as a whole. It almost offends them because they want their students to lead positively. The teachers are integral in the process of teaching leadership to students who had no leadership the previous year.

There is a different scenario with eighth graders in their home life. They are usually doing battle with their parents. Teachers many times will hear a different story about their students' behavior at home. They will tell parents how much they appreciate their child and the great attributes they bring to the class as a whole, and the parents might roll their eyes. This is classic, where a parent will ask if you are serious, then tell a different story about their behavior at home. This is attributed to them emerging as young men and women.

Effective teachers are much more likely to enjoy an eighth grade student than their parents.

Eighth grade students are more mature than early middle school. They can carry on a conversation like an adult. They are an absolute joy to have in a classroom. Eighth grade teachers shoulder the responsibility to make sure their students are ready for high school. They embrace middle school and know their students are not Jr. High. They are literally responsible for taking these students from seventh grade to high school in a year. It is a monumental task and a beautiful thing to witness when they are effective.

After the brutality of testing, the year ends with traditional ceremonies, dances, and trips they look forward to all year. Eighth grade students in an effective middle school usually do not get in trouble at the end of the year because they are looking forward to all of the positive activities and traditions at the school. If the eighth grade teachers have prepared their students, they will be ready for high school. If the middle school administration has done their job throughout the three-year experience of middle school, the students will have fond memories of this time of their life. They will feel safe, loved, and ready for their new adventure in high school.

One word consistently used by middle school teachers describing their students is *malleable*. They are still at the point where you can affect them. They are not too set in their ways and a teacher can easily have an impact on them academically and personally. They are drawn to excitement. You can see a change when you are able to reach their learning style. If a teacher is excited about a lesson, the students get excited about the lesson. If a teacher loves a subject, the students show interest in their subject. They can have a little success and ride it all the way to their personal best. They can come to you beat down or frustrated and you can actually see progress. We consistently talk about how far some of our eighth grade students have come over two years. The right teacher in a student's life can make the difference in the attitude towards academics and confidence level entering high school.

There are students who can be saved at this level. You can see their attitude adjust when you get to know them. They are constantly changing and looking to the adults in their life to show them how to react in situations. It is amazing how much more influence a teacher has on the lives of some of their students as opposed to their parents. I cannot tell you how many times a student has said, "That is what my dad says." However, they are suddenly taking the advice seriously. I also cannot tell you how many times parents have asked me to back them up because they listen to what I say. There is a short window that teachers have to make a major impact on these students and the window is wide open in middle school.

This brings back the importance of the right teachers filling the positions in middle school. The middle school teacher has a major impact during the most influential time of a child's life. The days should be long past that middle school positions are just filled by those who can't fit in elsewhere, temporary positions until they find their fit. Or even worse, a placement of punishment until a teacher will quit. There are gifted individuals who are needed in middle schools in every city and town. Their importance cannot be understated. The impact they have on students could change a students' direction over a lifetime.

Are you in the middle? Should you be in the middle? If the description of the students does not strike a level of fear in you, you are definitely middle school material. Do you relate to a particular grade level? Once you are a middle school teacher, your life will never be the same.

THREE

THE QUALITIES

There are countless qualities of great middle school teachers. The following italicized sentences highlight some of the top qualities that describe the best middle school teachers. Every teacher has unique qualities that are specific and contribute to their call.

By far, the most important quality of any teacher at any grade level is their character. Teachers must have good character. During an interview last spring with a very quiet but competent math candidate, I got to the last question, "Do you have any questions of me?" She responded with "Yes, I do. What makes your school the best place to work?" I was taken back. I had her daughter at school. Didn't she know about our building? This wasn't just a candidate; it was a parent. I had to take a breath before I answered. I said, "We are the best school because we seek people who are called to be in their positions. We make every attempt to connect with all of our students. Student interests come before adult interests in our building. Madison is the best place to work because we are looking for the best candidates who have a high level of character because these adults have a major impact on our students." She looked at me, smiled and said "Thank you, I thought so."

It took me by surprise. I knew I wanted teachers of character, but I am not for sure I had ever verbalized that publicly. I also had to think if it was okay to say that. It goes beyond the fact that we don't want to be on the news because a teacher has questionable character and did something bad, we have a responsibility to the students we serve to hire the best role models. We can't just put anyone in front of a middle school child. Character doesn't just mean they obey the law. Character means honesty at all times. Character means integrity. They are great people even when they are not at school. Character means faithful. Character means they treat others with respect. Character means they are in the right places. An educator's life is on display for the whole world to see and they have the most influential eyes watching their every move. Teachers can be humbled when they realize their character influences their students. Students blindly follow a teacher because of their position. Teachers should always display high moral character.

Beyond Character, the most important quality of a middle school teacher is the ability to develop genuine, healthy relationships with students. This is also the go-to statement for every speaker and know-it-all guru I have heard. Nobody can argue that you need to develop relationships, but it goes much deeper than just saying you have developed relationships. They cannot be fake. You must be genuine. A middle school student will see right through someone who is not genuine. You cannot fake smile at a middle school student and expect them not to read through it. You have to mean it when you smile. I can assure you they will know the difference. Relationships are key to a student's education.

Middle school students need to know that you like them. Every person needs to feel accepted, no matter the age. A high school student can go to a class and like the teacher without ever feeling like the teacher liked them. They can think the teacher is funny or the content might pique their interest. I take nothing away from the importance of developing relationships in high school or from the hard work of high school teachers to know their material, but middle school is a different story. If a middle school student does not think you like them, they take it personally. A high school student can use it as fuel to prove you wrong and pass your class. Even great middle school students will struggle in a class if they perceive a teacher does not like them. A middle school student will let you know if they think you do not care about them.

So why is it important to like a middle school student? They have to know you like them before you can develop a relationship with them. These students are going through the biggest change they will ever experience. In a matter of three years, most of them will rapidly grow and develop. They are all going through puberty and assaulted by hormones every day. They are not sure if they like themselves, and they need security that they are okay. If they look in to the eyes of a teacher and see that they are accepted, just as they are (which is crazy), all of their anxiety dissipates. When you comfort a middle school child, it is like standing outside and watching a storm clear up in a few seconds. The sun starts shining and the world is safe again. On the other side of that coin, if you do not like a child, the storm will continue to grow. Everyone remembers the trauma of their middle school years and have no desire to return.

Get to know them if you don't like them. As a teacher, I did not have any regrets on whether I had done enough to reach a student. I reached almost every student from every demographic. I gave it a shot with each child and found very few I couldn't find some sort of common ground. I truly cared about my students and gained personal satisfaction knowing that I positively affected them daily. When I became an assistant principal it became much more difficult to develop relationships with all of my students. I had gone from 100 to 600. I had also gone from teacher to school disciplinarian. I can honestly say that any student who I had taken the time to get to know, and developed some form of a relationship,

I had zero problems with their discipline. However, I usually had a disciplinary interaction with them before I knew them. Consider a girl I will call Ashley. Ashley moved from the other side of town and joined our middle school mid-semester. I saw her in the hallway, outside of her seventh grade science classroom and asked her why she was in the hall. She rolled her eyes and said something about the teacher being stupid, to which I swiftly corrected her assessment of MY teacher. I made my point, and I was right, but I knew it wasn't going to go well with this student in the future if I did not get to know her. Although I knew that I was right and obviously she was wrong, I still knew the situation could have been handled differently. I stopped about halfway down the hallway and walked back. I introduced myself, which I had not done before, and asked her where she came from. She spouted back to me the name of her previous school as if I was truly annoying her and she had something better to do. I then asked her who she lived with and why they moved. She just stared at me for a moment. I told her that I really needed to get to know her a little bit and that I did not like our previous interaction. She then spilled out a story of divorce and an absent biological father. We talked for a while in the hallway and then I thanked her for sharing a little bit of her life with me. I knew I would see her in the future with teacher discipline referrals and it was extremely important that she know that I like her and am interested in her well-being if she were going to allow me to help her be successful. I still do this frequently.

Find something unique about each child. If you find something unique in children, it will help you appreciate them. Some students play an instrument and some students can sing. Other students will play a sport. No matter what the scenario, each child is unique and you need to find out why they are unique. When you find out something about them, you can then ask them about their situation and begin to relate. Middle school students do not care if you understand what it means to sit in the first chair of band or orchestra. They don't care if you know that a linebacker is the offense or defense of the football team. What they care about is if you are interested in listening to what is important to them. When you learn something individual about each student, it becomes more difficult not to take interest in their well-being, thus you begin to care about them and like them.

Effective middle school teachers put student interest first. When planning a lesson, student learning is the only objective. Quality instructors will go to whatever lengths possible to make a lesson come alive. They will don a silly costume or fake an accent or do a cheer; it doesn't matter the potential personal embarrassment if it means a student will learn. When there is a discipline issue, the teacher puts the student interest before his own. Great teachers swallow their pride every day in the best interest of their pupils. Students get to start over the next day because that is what is best for the student. When there is a parent meeting, student success is the purpose. Every meeting focuses on student success. Every procedure in the school will focus on student safety and learning. Students are the focal point of every day in the life of great educators. Having that understanding with a group of other educators makes it that much easier to work together.

Another important quality of a teacher is their ability to laugh. If a teacher has a sense of humor, she can diffuse almost any situation. A typical middle school student is always on the brink of laughing either with you or at you. One of the first reactions when you are constantly aware of your surroundings and scared that anyone will acknowledge you for any reason is to laugh. When you laugh, you release endorphins that cause a euphoria and an ability to relax. In other words, they self-medicate by laughing. If you ask a student why they like a teacher, their answers are "because they love us" and "because they are funny". You don't even have to be funny to get a giggle out of a middle school student. Middle school students love corny planned humor as well. A teacher can wear a funny hat and the students think it is great. You can use a voice inflection or an accent and it becomes an epic event. They will even remind you three years later. Middle school students get a kick out of just about anything. You also have to be able to laugh at yourself.

If you have ever taught middle school, you are aware of every imperfection in your life. I have a weekly bowling club that attracts an eclectic group of students. Generally, students actually want me to bowl with them. I enjoy getting out of the office right after school once a week to spend time with my group of students. One week, a group of sixth grade girls asked me to bowl with them. I generally like the competitive nature of some boys talking trash, but I obliged and bowled with the young ladies. Within about ten minutes the girls nonchalantly pointed out that I had a long face, I was balding and I had a knot on my forehead. They were right, and it was not the first time I have had those characteristics highlighted. You have to be able to laugh at yourself and move on or you will need medication. One day during my first year of teaching, I called the students over for direct instruction at the beginning of class. Someone talked me into putting jars full of water, marbles, and a plant on each table because some study showed that it was a best practice. I had asked the students to move to the board for direct instruction, which means forty students moved their chairs over to the whiteboard where I could prepare them for the days' lesson. I was in the middle of instructing the students when I leaned on the table. You can guess what happened next: the table tilted, the water spilled out, ran down the table and covered my pants. When the marbles hit the floor, it sounded like a waterfall. The water seeped through my pants and it was cold. I guarantee you my face showed that it was a shock to my system. Forty students sat silent momentarily until they saw the look on my face. I just smiled. They broke in to laughter for a good five minutes. I really wanted to just run out of the room and get cleaned up, but you have to be able to laugh at yourself in middle school. I taught the rest of the hour with wet pants and a group of students who kept grinning at me. I have found over time that it is much better to laugh with them.

Middle school teachers exemplify patience. Middle

school teachers are gifted with a level of patience to stay sane in this world they have embraced. Students will forget what you just told them, not on purpose, but because they literally were distracted the moment they left your presence. Students will inadvertently get in your bubble. They are the definition of close-talkers. They will test every boundary. Middle school teachers have to prepare themselves to be patient in the midst of storms. Everyone loses their patience at some point and most regret the outcome. These students require a level of patience that only a gifted professional can provide.

Middle school teachers also have to exert a level of patience with the parents they encounter. The students are a little easier to extend patience to since they have the adolescent excuse. Parents typically believe they are still dealing with that responsible child they had come to appreciate in upper elementary. When the parent calls asking why the teacher had lost their student's paper or why they had not informed their child of an assignment, the teachers must exert a level of patience while explaining to the parent the new creature living in their home. Most parents stay in the denial stage of mourning their perfect child they lost in sixth grade.

Middle school educators communicate consistently. Middle school educators must be comfortable with communicating. When you are in middle school, you are literally in the middle of everyone. You are between elementary and high school. You will communicate with both levels constantly. You are in the middle of students and their parents because this crazy person has just decided to take over their child's body and they need someone to speak their language. The students need you to interpret for the parents as well. Middle school educators at effective middle schools communicate with each other multiple times a day. The better the communication between teachers on a team, the better we serve our students. Teachers should be communicating through planned meetings that serve a purpose. Teachers have to be able to communicate with students. This is not always easy as they are all different. Some students are going to make themselves known and some students are extremely introverted at this age. The majority do not want to stand out and need the teacher to attempt to communicate daily.

Another important quality of a middle school teacher is to play with the students. When teachers are young, and sometimes when they are seasoned, they can get on a playground and keep up with the students. I found my way down to the P.E. class many times during my seven years of teaching. I even found my way down to the gym class as an assistant principal. Even now, during lunch/recess, I will play four square, tetherball, or throw a football with the students as often as possible. I even talk trash to the amusement of the students. We have teachers who will come out and play games with students. Some middle school educators are scared to go on a playground or a gym class. It shows character that you are willing to hang out with them on their turf. Middle school students love it when you play games with them. They see you in a completely different way after you spend time outside of the regular classroom. They go home and tell their parents about it. When you play with a student, it creates a great opportunity to get to know them.

Playing with your students doesn't have to stop at the door. Play an academic game in class. Make it active. Use flyswatters to hit the correct term on the board, use buzzers to give the right answer, or play academic bingo. The point is, play with the students. Dress up as a character from history one day. Plan a day with the team for everyone to dress up in character. As an eighth grade teacher, we held a month long civil war simulation activity. It culminated with one Civil War day where all students dressed up from the era, but we had students dressing up daily with hats and jackets. We also had simulations for Lewis and Clark, the Underground Railroad, the Gold Rush, and several others. Students need to be active in class. If you are reading a book in class, dress up as the character. The students in middle school will appreciate a dress up day more than any age group. Students will remember when they are actively learning. They actually forget they are learning because they are having fun playing.

Quality instructors admit they do not know it all and are far from perfect. I know it sounds crazy, but teachers sometimes bear the burden of pretending they know everything. Let go of that burden quickly. As a history teacher, I consistently heard the comment, "You didn't know that?", when referring to anything that has ever happened in the world at any time. I dispelled that notion very quickly. I taught American History (1757-1860) and I couldn't even begin to tell you that I knew everything about that time period, but I loved it. I enjoyed every bit of knowledge I could retain and much of it came from students. I also taught English. I let the students know I am really good, but not perfect, at grammar. When you let the students know they are experts who have experiences and information that can contribute to the class, it makes you a facilitator of learning where all can contribute.

A great quality of a teacher is the ability to know when to ignore. Some people call it thick skin. Sometimes it is simple discernment. You have to ignore the attitudes students will give you when you challenge them academically. You have to ignore when students decide to notice every flaw. Great teachers know when to fight battles and when to ignore unintentional behaviors. They know when to ignore the moans and groans of their students. Sometimes they ignore the roll of the eyes and smirks when giving homework. When students realize you care enough about their education to not waste their time on a "free day" they begin to respect the intentions. Every day is important. There are battles you will want to fight that are worth winning, but ignoring the minor battles is a talent great teachers possess.

Great teachers are passionate. Most people are passionate about something, but middle school teachers are passionate about student learning. They want the students to know what it means to love a subject. An English teacher wants their students to love reading. If they were honest, they could truly care less about whether they can regurgitate the right information on a test one day of the year. They are much happier to find their students love reading. They want their students to express themselves with creative writing. A science teacher leads their students through as many labs as possible because they want their students to explore, ask questions and find the answers through inquiry. A middle school history teacher dresses in character and comes up with simulations and reenactments in hopes their students can identify with history, understand where we came from, and explore the past with an appetite and thirst for more knowledge. Math teachers know they must make their students understand how this is applicable for their daily life. It is more than just a subject to learn, it is a need for students to experience the curriculum. They want them to find a passion for learning. Students are drawn to the passions and excitement of their teachers. Passionate people are contagious, and teachers know their students will want to learn when they are learning with the students. Passionate teachers never weary of learning with their students. Every great teacher will tell their students they are still learning every day.

Middle school teachers are kid magnets. It doesn't matter your age, teachers are drawn to students, and students are drawn to their teachers. It could be because the students feel welcomed and cared about. It could be because, unlike the average adult, the teacher is not scared of a group of adolescents. When a middle school teacher walks in to the cafeteria, they are welcomed by a mass of their students. When the teacher walks down the hallway, students will greet and high five the teacher. When a teacher enters Walmart, they are spotted and mobbed like a movie star. When teachers go to a football game on a Friday night, they are greeted and treated as if those students hadn't seen them in months. Teachers who excel in middle school welcome this attention not because it feels good but because they know with every high five and every hug, they are building relationships with their students.

Great middle school teachers are invested. They take the time to go to a game. Sometimes it is not the game of choice for that educator, but they go anyway. I do not particularly love softball and the season is brutally hot, but I will go see my students play when I know it is important to them. I will cheer them with passion because if I make it out there in that brutal heat, they had better give it their all. I have been to weightlifting competitions, every traditional sport you can imagine, and even a barrel riding competition. Great teachers have been to band, orchestra and choir concerts. They cannot and do not attend everything because it would be exhausting and emotionally unhealthy, but great teachers pick and choose the right opportunities to show their students they are interested in their life.

Middle school teachers stay interested. They refuse to get bored. Middle schools are typically never boring with the activity of this age group, but curriculum can get mundane if you continue to reuse the old lessons. The best teachers are constantly discovering new ways to learn information. Although some successful lesson plans can be duplicated, good teachers aren't afraid to try something new. Reinventing the wheel is a good thing when the teacher is bored with the same old lesson plan.

The best teachers reach out to everyone. It is impossible to shoulder the responsibility to reach every student, but the best teachers make every effort. They greet all of their students every day at the door. They take the opportunity to look all of their students in the eye at least one time that day and shake a hand or give a high five. They use different techniques to involve them in class. These teachers have procedures in place to call on all students regularly and give them the chance to answer. They physically make their way around a room daily to check on students. They do not let a behavior problem take over and get the negative attention of a classroom, nor do they allow the teacher's pet to take all of the positive attention. They know the learning styles of their students and seek to meet them. Great teachers learn about their students and their families. They seek to help them in any way possible. They want nothing more than to see a genuine smile on every student's face before they leave their classroom each day because they were able to reach them.

Most people are drawn to others similar to themselves. Teachers aren't any different. I realized this my entry year of teaching. Students were from all four sides of town equally and wore uniforms. I did not know where any students were from until we began to talk about their elementary schools. The majority of the kids that I became so quickly attached were from elementary schools near the neighborhood where I was raised. Upon this discovery, I made an intentional effort to reach out to different cultures and every student. Although I was not consciously choosing to relate to students with whom I shared a culture, I was naturally drawn to them. I began asking more questions and consciously conversing with students who had not migrated to me. I found great satisfaction in diversifying my relationships with all students. It is the desire of quality educators to reach all students.

Are you in the middle? Do these qualities match you as a teacher? Do these qualities seem like a challenge or a way of life? Middle school students need the best teachers to answer "yes" to the call to teach. They need teachers with high moral character and great qualities to enrich their lives.

FOUR

THE HEROES

Superhero apparel has become a commonplace sighting in almost every setting. At one time, you would only see a super hero costume on Halloween or the big screen. You might have even seen someone on TV behind an announcer who wants attention wearing a superman costume. People talk about superheroes and the need for their powers. Today, I can walk through the hallways of my middle school any day of the week and find students wearing shirts, jackets, and hoodies paying tribute to the worlds' fictitious super heroes. I would like to say that it is a fad, but students have been wearing superhero clothing since Michael Keaton played Batman in the late 80's.

Obviously, there isn't anyone who has super heroic powers like those portrayed in the movies, but there are heroes who make an immediate impact on this world because they did something miraculous at the right moment. For some it is a choice, putting themselves out there using their skills to help someone in a crisis. Police officers put themselves in harm's way to help those who are in need. With the amount of drugs and mental illness that police officers face every day, I cannot imagine being in their shoes. I have a friend who is a highway patrol officer. When we were young, he would pick me up and take me on patrol. He is 6'4" and weighed at least 260. He played football at the college I attended and I witnessed him be a hero on multiple occasions. Patrolman Branson Perry is a man among men when it came to those threatening the innocent. He is a personable teddy bear to those who need to be comforted. He has skills that give him the opportunity to help those in need. He is a hero.

Arguably, the most popular hero in our culture is the firefighter. They are trained to save the innocent. Everyone is innocent in a fire, so they are beloved in our society. I spoke to a former DHS employee who told me that he would ride a fire truck to a home in a rough neighborhood, where kids were in danger, because everyone loved the firefighters and he felt safe with their transport. When I was a child, everyone told me that police officers and firefighters were heroes. The popularity of firefighters has continued to increase over the years. Firefighters risk their lives to save people. It is not uncommon to see firefighters get hurt. They are usually the first on the scene when there is an emergency, and they don't hesitate to help. We love firefighters because they will help us the moment we need them. They are not threatening to anyone. Most people agree firefighters are everyday heroes.

Another hero of our society is the military service member. I can't think of anyone more deserving of our appreciation than those who risk their lives for our freedom. I am grateful that this generation, regardless of political affiliation, has embraced the soldiers in our military. They are fighting for the cause of freedom throughout the world and deserve our support. They don't choose where they go, they just serve. On the playground in 2007, I got a call from a former student. I was an assistant principal in charge of all discipline and playground duties. The caller was a young woman serving in our military in Afghanistan. I had known her in middle school but hadn't spoken with her in several years. She called to let me know where she was stationed and share some of her experiences. She also called to say thank you. That was by far the longest distance call I had ever received. I was so proud to know that she gave up her immediate plans for college to join the military in a time of war. I am pretty sure I was about three inches taller walking in from that playground, I was so swelled with joy. Each soldier is a hero for our country.

I could name many heroes in our society. Most of the time clergy, charities, and nonprofit organizations invest in the lives of our community. They run children's programs, feed the hungry and try to help those in need. The majority of the time it is a thankless job. There are many who run shelters and food kitchens. There are elements of society that some people serve that the majority never encounter. These people are unsung heroes in our society. They will not make the news and they will rarely be shown appreciation, but they are definitely helping and saving others.

Teachers have been heroes in our society for well over a century. It is not uncommon for an athlete to attribute their success to a teacher or coach. Teachers have been accredited for the success of authors, astronauts, musicians and any other occupation, whether it be glamorous or not. Teachers have the opportunity for the greatest impact on our society. Teachers are the front line in our classrooms that see students for seven hours a day. Students will spend more time with their teachers than with their family while in school.

Schools are a microcosm of society, and teachers get to experience all elements of society. They will get to know the families of their students. Teachers also begin to clue in on why their students act and react. It doesn't take long for clarity to emerge when dealing with parents. Students either take parental authority seriously because they have backed it up with discipline over the years, or they pretend to care until they leave your presence because their parents have never enforced anything. You will begin to understand which students are playing those games. Teachers experience the poor, middle class and wealthy. They deal with classy and classless people. Teachers learn the different cultures and religions of their students. When you immerse yourself in to the lives of the community through the classroom, you experience life through the eyes of all your students. This viewpoint will most definitely cause compassion for circumstances and patience for behaviors. When the students see that you truly understand them, they know you care for them. Barriers will break down and they will trust you.

I know effective teachers are heroes when they answer the call to serve. Rarely will a teacher be required to give CPR, pull a child from flames, or save them from gunfire. A lifetime of teaching will probably not bring one of those tragic circumstances, but teachers have an opportunity to be a hero daily. Although many people in our society are able to save lives and protect freedom, teachers are able to make a difference in the lives of students on a consistent basis. Teachers instruct students academically; they have the opportunity to display good character as a role model; and they are able to counsel their students on a daily basis. Just like police, servicemen and fireman, it comes at a pay much less than the movie stars who display fictitious heroics on the big screen.

Most of the glamour of actual heroism is lost when it comes to reality. I have had countless students tell me their dad is their hero. It isn't a matter of a one-time event, it is a daily lifestyle of nurture and stability. Most of the time heroism is someone who has met a need that nobody else was going to meet. It may or may not be life or death. It may just be something that comes naturally for an individual. It is much easier to snap in to action in a one-time event than to be there every day for a student. A hero for a student could be someone who was patient enough to teach them the skills they would use later in their life.

"Those who can't do, teach." I am not sure where this quote originated, but in my world, it couldn't be farther from the truth. If you cannot understand how to handle a middle school student, you will gladly get a job somewhere else. Many who can indeed teach because it makes a difference in the lives of their students. You see it on their faces when they light up. There are teachers who make lessons come alive.

Students remember those lessons forever. There are teachers who figure out the learning style of their students, so they can begin to understand the content. People remember when the light bulb came on and who flipped the switch. There are teachers who give up their planning period or lunch to help students. There are teachers who stay after school to tutor students. Those teachers are heroes. Try to find someone in the workforce who works extra hours without pay because people need him or her. You will see that daily in an effective middle school.

Many professionals will attribute their love for a subject to a favorite teacher. A teacher helped them discover their gift in math or their curiosity for history. A teacher may help a child find himself through writing, or lose herself in a sonata. Sometimes people make a living in the subject area of their favorite teacher. Sometimes it is just a hobby. Occasionally, they really weren't that interested in the subject as much as the teacher's passion for the subject. One thing is certain: that subject came alive because there was a teacher who made it come alive for their students.

Although I am grateful for those who save lives in an instant, others spend their day making the small differences. Some give a smile every day to a student who never receives a smile in the evening. There are people who stop an individual from committing suicide. There are people who help prevent individuals from getting to that point of depression. The heroism of teachers will always be understated because they rarely know the difference they have made.

My uncle Ted worked for the River Authority on the Ohio River. He engineered pieces of metal that could help dams close and bridges move. He also taught at a technology school nearby. Since I am in education, he would constantly talk about the students he had in class over 30 years ago. He would tell me how he handled situations and then tell me that he probably wouldn't be able to be a teacher in today's society. He remembered his students, almost all boys. He would tell me about their life and how he cared for all of them.

He wanted to see them be successful in life. My uncle was a sailor. There are many stories told of his time on a ship. He was a straightforward man who did not shy away from his beliefs. When John Glenn orbited the moon, he landed in the ocean upon his return. My uncle pulled John Glenn out of the water. About 20 years later, they recognized this act of heroism and named a street after him in Belpre, Ohio. At Uncle Teds' funeral, a man who wanted to let me know how my uncle affected his life approached me. It wasn't John Glenn. A former tech student told me several stories about how Ted took him hunting with the family. Several more former students told stories about my uncle. He took them hunting and fishing after school. He went to their ballgames. He took people out to buy them shoes because they didn't have any money. Uncle Ted didn't have any money either. He found employment for several of his former students. Uncle Ted was not a teacher by trade; it was not his choice of occupation. Teaching part-time was a blip in his life. The impact he made on his students brought them to his funeral three decades later. None were sad; they just wanted the family to know he made a difference.

If there is a need, an effective educator will notice and seek opportunities to provide. I know a teacher who spends hundreds of dollars each year on clothes for her students. We have never spoken about it, but others let me know. There are teaching teams who adopt students every year for Christmas and seek to meet their needs. Teachers know when a student doesn't have a jacket. Teachers notice when a child is dirty and needs clean clothes. Teachers know when a student doesn't have enough to eat. Sometimes they help feed them; sometimes they connect their family with the right agency. There are dozens of agencies ready to help the needy that are dependent on educators to help them connect. There is a non profit in our town that packs a bag full of grocery items for students every week. Our counselors connect the families to the agency through teacher recommendations. Each week, several dozen students go home with a bag full of nutritious foods they depend on to make it through the weekend.

Effective middle schools care enough about their children and their families to link them to the appropriate resources. Sometimes it takes more than just connecting them to an agency. Many times it is tough conversations that must take place in the best interest of the student.

In middle school there are physical changes that happen to children. Without graphic detail, we all know the absolute funk even the best-groomed child can emit into the atmosphere. There may not be anything worse than being in a room with 28 seventh graders after a warm afternoon recess. The students seem oblivious, but it is torture on the adults. Most parents will recognize and intervene to buy deodorant, force a shower twice a day and take any other precautions to let their child know about hygiene. They love their children enough to let them know they stink. There are students, boys and girls, who never get that level of parental love. It is left to other adults to intervene. If that student attends an effective middle school, with a team of teachers who love them, one of them will agree to confront the situation. They will even buy them the needed items to be clean and smell good. There is a special crown in heaven for the counselors and educators who confront these situations daily. They are unsung heroes.

If an educator is aware that a student is experiencing neglect or abuse, they are responsible to call DHS. In order to know that a child is experiencing neglect or abuse, you have to know the student very well. Students don't bleed embarrassing personal information to very many people. They will reach out when they think that someone will have the answers they need. I have been a part of many calls to DHS. As an administrator, I know every call made in my building. I make sure that an administrator or counselor is there for the interview with the child. During my teaching career, one call stood out above the rest. A girl approached me to let me know she and her mother were going to be leaving together and running away from her mother's boyfriend. This would be her last day at this school. She decided to let me and an assistant teacher know that she would miss us. As I prodded her for more information, she made us aware that her mothers boyfriend had touched her inappropriately. We called DHS immediately and were pushed out of the way as they did a full investigation. The situation was way out of my league and I believed the damage would be too much for this young lady. As details emerged, the abuse was much worse than we thought, and had been going on for over a year. She stayed enrolled in our school and I had her for the remainder of her 8th grade year. She was very poor, but DHS still got her the needed counseling services. She updated us frequently about counseling. Even when she was in high school, she would come back to talk to me and the assistant teacher who made that call. She completely forgave the man who had harmed her and held no resentment because she got the appropriate counseling. She was a whole young woman before leaving high school. I was amazed at what a difference a great counselor could make on a student. As a teacher, I had to call DHS several times. I didn't want to call because it took the situation out of my control, and I didn't want the student to lose trust, however I obeyed the law. I witnessed lives turned upside down, but students landed on their feet and out of the tragic situation they were experiencing. I witnessed damaged lives made whole again through a change in environment and counseling. As a teacher, I felt that personal gratification knowing I had made a difference. Students come back and thank teachers, not for making a call, but for noticing.

Effective educators are in classrooms and hallways every day connecting with students. They notice need, neglect and abuse because they know their students. They are the bridge to get these students the help they need. They make the call home to ask if they need assistance to get their children clothes. They find out if they have enough food in their home. They ask parents, who probably don't wear deodorant themselves if they know their children smell. These phone calls require sensitivity and thick skin because it embarrasses most people. The initial reaction from many parents is defensive and hateful. Educators have to show compassion so parents will allow them to help. Teachers notice changes in students and ask the right questions. They are trusted with the deepest secrets of their students. They betray student trust by informing authorities because they care enough about the child's safety. These actions show the greatest compassion for the well-being of children. These efforts are nothing short of heroic, and it happens daily across America in effective middle schools.

Superheroes solve a problem in an instant. They are quick to swoop in and fix huge problems. The end is in sight if we can just turn the knob or hit this button. This is the opposite of what educators do each day. There is rarely a super hero fix to the huge problems in life. Students are drawn to that imaginary fix, where their life is suddenly okay. They are now normal. They can pass a class, talk to a girl, go home safely or confidently hit the ball. Effective educators know the end is rarely in sight. They stay patient and work with their students daily through the journey of life, seeking to help them solve their problems. Effective educators model lifelong learning and problem solving for their students.

Effective educators want their students to have skills necessary for a productive life. Effective schools have programs in place that teach life skills systematically. Honesty, integrity, faithfulness, compassion, respect, and many other skills are modeled and taught. In middle school, social skills are the focal point. It is a necessity with students who are figuring out boundaries and how to treat others. Life skills are not limited to social. I knew a gym teacher who had girls consistently come to her to help them lose weight and have a healthy lifestyle. They would come to her privately and she would help them weigh themselves. Mrs. Hotaling would give them a pedometer and encourage them to take a certain amount of steps per day. She would work with them on their diet to give them healthier options. She would keep them accountable because they trusted her enough to seek her help. Mrs. Hotaling was trusted with the most sensitive subject in life: the weight of a female. Men and boys are sensitive about obesity, but early adolescent females are completely unapproachable. Mrs.

Hotaling taught them life skills they needed and will use for the rest of their lives. She gave them confidence to confront an issue that affects their health and quality of life. She will be a hero to those girls for a lifetime.

I have the privilege to work with Sonja Jenner who teaches a program named Vision Quest. It is an alternative program designed to catch kids who are falling through the cracks. Most of them did not pass their state exams the previous year and have been identified by their teachers as needing a safety net or Sonja in their life. I have concluded that nobody can fill this position like Sonja Jenner. I have seen multiple people try, but none can reach these students like she can. It is a gift. I have attempted to convince her to make a dummies guide for her class. She has close to fifteen seventh and eighth graders report to her for several core classes and one elective class. During their elective with Mrs. Jenner, she teaches life skills, character traits and service. She communicates with the majority of teachers in the building on a consistent basis to get updates on her students' behavior and academics. She takes the kids once a month to a food pantry to serve those in need. She has multiple community service opportunities they complete after school. Former teachers, parents and other students notice the change that a commitment to her class will bring to her students. They are blessed to have such a person committed to their success. Sonja is a meek and kind individual who tells a wonderful story of growing up in South Dakota. She has three grown daughters with her husband, who is an amazing high school teacher. She has been in the same building for 30 years and continuously keeps a fire burning to affect the lives of her students. She is a hero, not only to her students, but also to her community. She has frequent visitors of past students. Some of them rough, some of them successful, but all of them know they owe her a lifetime of gratefulness. She invested in their lives and nothing can repay what she has given to them. She has answered a call on her life to work with middle level students who need her skillset. Sonja doesn't seek recognition. She has been nominated for teacher of the year for nine straight years and will not accept the nomination for fear the paperwork will consume her time. She wants to focus whole-heartedly on her students.

Effective teachers make every day matter. These teachers do not stop when technology doesn't work. They do not have free days where there is no academic value. If there is a party, it is curriculum-related. They did not enter this profession to waste their time; they answered the call to make a difference. They invest every day because they want their students to be successful in life and they know they have a limited amount of time to reach their students.

Effective teachers do not stop their efforts when the students are promoted. Teachers leave themselves open to students when they need to return. Students returning to their former middle school to see teachers is a daily occurrence at effective middle schools. For many, those teachers filled the role of parent or mentor, and those students still have a need for their approval. They are part of the foundation of their students' life. Effective teachers are called to their position and are heroes in our society.

There has been much attention given recently to legacy. There have been multitudes of books that have included the topic. It has been covered from both secular and religious viewpoints. Individuals begin to realize they are mortal, and they want to be remembered. People want their lives to mean something. For many athletes, it means they make the Hall of Fame. For many famous people in general, they start a charity or hold an event. For some people, it is a position or making partner in their firm.

A teacher will not receive a lavish retirement party with the car of their dreams, a trip to Hawaii, and a huge payday. They will be lucky to get some cake with former students and friends. A close friend of mine, Steve Ham, gave me a pretty hard picture of retirement. He said, "There won't even be students in that building who remember you in two years. What you do right now is what you will be remembered for." Being a retired middle school band teacher, he knew the reality.

A teacher's legacy is lived out through their students. They work hard and invest in the lives of young people. Students remember the teachers who cared about what they taught. Students remember the teachers who cared about them. The investment is not lost on people. Lives are changed every day in the classroom. Teachers get to enjoy what they do every day and live a life knowing they made a difference. Their legacy is their students. Most educators could care less if you name a building after them. There are buildings everywhere named after people we don't even know. They would much rather get a card from a former student. Effective teachers who answer the call to teach do not have regrets on their legacy. The legacy of a teacher is that they had the opportunity to be a hero every day and their effect on students will live out for generations.

Did you ever imagine heroics being part of your job description? Were you aware that you would be idolized? Can you imagine the impact of a lifetime of teaching?

FIVE

THE TYPE

The type of person who is called to be a middle school teacher varies like the characters walking down the street. When perusing downtown on a busy day, you see all types of people. The same is to be said for middle level educators. There is no "type of person" who teaches. Great middle school teachers come from all walks of life. They look and act differently. In the building I work, there are the very expressive and very reserved. Some teachers have a city background; some have a country background. Some teachers are coaches; some have never played a sport. I have teachers who would be considered very strict and some that are much more laid back. There is a balance between male and female. They range in age from 23-60. One thing is certain: all teachers believe they are in the right place. Each knows it is their responsibility to reach out to students. This is the only thing they all have in common.

In conversations with other administrators, there is a belief that everyone should fall in to a particular personality type. One administrator said that he would hire all coaches if he could. He also believed that if you were in administration, you should have a coaching background. I have also heard building leaders say that they wish they could just start all over with a building full of fresh college graduates. I couldn't disagree more.

I had my eyes opened to the "one type fits all and saves the school" mentality very early in my career. I tried to connect with every student when I began teaching. I don't just mean to know their name and teach the objectives. I was truly frustrated that I didn't have enough time or opportunity to get to know every student personally. I cherish the ability to affect lives and I thought if there were just enough time in a day, I could reach them all.

I was wrong. There are some students that you can reach, and there are others who need someone else to reach them. Some teachers are really popular and get to know many of their students. One day I assigned my students a writing prompt that drew some interesting responses. They had to describe their favorite teacher and they couldn't choose me. Many responses were predictable because I knew the staff. I knew which teachers the kids thought hung the moon. One of the essays caught my attention. A student chose a very quiet and unassuming para teacher whom she had developed a relationship through Civil War committees. She spent several weeks with her in the Ladies Aid Committee, where they had sewn blankets for soldiers. Only a few girls would join this committee each year, but this para teacher was obviously very effective with those girls. She described how much this para teacher had positively affected her life. She wrote several pages about her appreciation for the impact this para teacher had on her. I didn't know anyone outside of the 8th grade staff knew this adult existed. As hard as I tried, I couldn't find anything in common with this young lady. However, she made a connection to this para teacher.

How bland would a school be if it only had one type of teacher? I hear the comment, "I wish all teachers were like 'insert name'," all of the time. In that statement, we underscore the many teachers who make a difference to other students. It is impossible for one teacher to reach all students.

It is also pretentious for anyone to believe he can reach all students. There isn't a personality style or a manual that can take a teacher to a universal ability to reach every child.

I work with coaches who do an exceptional job in the classroom. They put their classroom responsibilities before any after school coaching duties. However, many coaches have a similar attitude and demeanor. For someone to believe one personality type can reach all students in a building has blinders on to the people who have the skills and call on their life to reach students. For those who believe we should hire all brand new, fresh out of college, untainted and excited young teachers to fill all classrooms demeans the importance of experience. Experienced teachers hold a wealth of knowledge on how to connect to students. They also can tell you what programs and curriculum have worked and failed in the past. It is important to keep seasoned professionals as long as they are still excited to be there. They are historians who can bring immense pride to an institution. I have a history teacher who has requested to be on the same team as a science teacher who taught him in middle school. He wants the opportunity to be mentored before he retires. Rick Johnson brings more to his class room every year and has embraced his role as a mentor. It is essential to have a healthy mix of all age groups, gender, and experience levels in a middle school.

We need all types of people to reach our students. I know two eighth grade science teachers who teach next door to each other. Each teacher is highly effective. They have polar opposite personalities and both work together to efficiently help the other. They understand their strengths and use them to help each other become stronger. One teacher is very vocal and does not know a stranger. She will tell you all about her lesson plans for the day. The other teacher is very reserved. If you walk in her classroom, she will show you her lesson plans and invite you to join a group where students are actively working. Both have structured and active classrooms. Students are consistently engaged. Both teachers have many students who consider them their favorite teacher. They are different inside and outside the classroom, but very effective with middle school students. It is important we understand it takes all types to reach all students.

As I navigate the halls of my school, I am amazed at the people who have committed this time of their life to invest in middle school students. There is a brilliant man who was the head of a college department for decades. There is a young lady, across the hall, who has skills beyond her years in dealing with all classroom situations. She is in her second year of teaching, but she knows how to differentiate instruction so sixth graders can stay focused. She is teamed with a thirty-year veteran whom she works with daily. The veteran has been in multiple districts and wanted to continue with middle school. It is her passion. A social studies teacher has his students acting out lessons quite often. I see a twenty-five-year veteran science teacher who stepped out of high school coaching and has more energy and excitement for the classroom than ever. He has a very structured environment, but has always connected with sixth graders. A Spanish teacher has the students speaking Spanish the first day of school. Upon entering his class, you will see students moving around in stations and answering questions in Spanish. Another teacher has reentered the profession after a fifteen-year layoff with children. She is very quiet, but in her math class she comes alive and the students love her and the content. Next to her, a history teacher has been in private and public schools. He reinvents the wheel consistently with his lesson plans, so he stays interested in the content. He loves to instruct but hates wasting his time in meetings. Next door to him is an English teacher who makes literature come alive. There are orchestra and band teachers who will recruit and work with all students. There is a choir teacher in his second year who integrates music and literacy. These teachers come from all over. It takes all of them to reach students.

There are students meant just for you. It is amazing when a student connects with you. Generally, you don't know until it happens. You will find out because a parent contacts you to let you know how much they appreciate your efforts in reaching their child. There are few greater feelings in this world than knowing you helped a child when nobody else seemed to be able to connect. At the middle school level, they need to connect to an adult. Friends are the most important thing in their lives, but they are still affected by adults. When you answer the call to teach, there will be students every year who connect to you. This huge responsibility is embraced by effective teachers.

When you see the effect you have on the lives of students, it is easy to forget your own needs. It is important that you protect your time and your stress level, so you can have longevity in your teaching career. Teachers must stay healthy, both physically and emotionally. A teacher must take the opportunity to be with family, limit their time working on the weekends, and take vacations so they keep their minds fresh.

If you are an educator or you accept the call to teach, do not let anyone burn you out. There are numerous responsibilities at a school. Everyone needs to do his part, but nobody needs to take on more than his share. It is important when teachers are where they know they are effective; they do not let others commit them to obligations that drain their energy. Teachers who are effective are excited every day. They enjoy their position and feel that they are contributing to the greater good. I have multiple teachers in my building who will jump if I tell them something is important. We have worked together on committees where we had a blast planning great things for our students. I have also witnessed great teachers begin to lose their joy because they have too many commitments. They begin to burn out because they are not as effective in the classroom. Administrators will easily commit a willing teacher to work on committees. Don't over commit to obligations that affect your classroom efficacy. Shed any responsibility or obligation as soon as it does not bring joy. Teachers who need to let loose some of the responsibilities they have taken on periodically request reprieve of those duties from me. I always reluctantly oblige because I know they need to be highly effective at their chosen position.

It is important to stick to what you are called to do. Develop your gifts. Enjoy every minute of your time in the classroom. Look up professional development opportunities that will enhance your abilities. Find others who teach in your content area and glean from their experience. Share your success stories. Get better every day. This is the reason you chose to teach.

Don't let someone talk you in to working in a subject or discipline where you do not feel called. I had a teacher who had the right certification for a position where a teacher was struggling. I asked her to switch disciplines mid-year. I had good reason, and it sounded great in theory. She said she would do anything I needed her to do. After a month, I knew I had made a mistake. She had gone from a joyous person excited every day entering the building to a stressed-out worker. Her smiles were few. She worked hard but was miserable. The next year I switched them back. She found her joy, and she was back to being an effective teacher in the content area where she was called.

I have made numerous comments to teachers to find out if they are truly happy. If someone gets a certification just to get their foot in the door, they will eventually burn out. You may have the ability to stretch yourself to a position that needs filled. However, your days will be long, and you will grow weary. Teach what you enjoy or find a place that will offer you that opportunity.

Don't burn out flying solo. There are many effective teachers working in ineffective schools. They are on an island and not working as a team with others. The structure of the school has caused them to fly solo and create miracles. Most of the time, these people are considered rock stars. They are the popular teacher. They save every kid they can possibly reach. Eventually, when you find yourself alone on an island, you burn out. Other teammates are not available, and you lose your passion. You realize you are not in an effective environment and everything is dependent on you. I was on an island my first year of teaching, and I knew I was good. I was a rock star in that building before I got out of the car. It was a depressing little place with a tyrant for a principal. Within a week, every student and adult in the community knew I had arrived. I was an energetic young man who expanded opportunities to reach learning styles. The students immediately thrived. The next year I was very fortunate to find a position closer to home. I began my career at Thoreau Demonstration Academy. When I arrived at Thoreau, I quickly learned I was just another great teacher in a highly effective building. The majority of the teachers at Thoreau were incredible. We were an effective team. To prove my point, most of those teachers have moved on to careers in administration, consulting or instructional coaching. Teachers who are also effective have replaced them. They are still a thriving school. My solution to those who are at ineffective schools: move to an effective school. If leadership is not hiring effective teachers, don't burn out; move to a school that puts students first, and you will thrive. If effective teachers all work together, it creates an ideal atmosphere for students. The schools where ineffective leadership is hiring ineffective teachers need to hire new leadership.

A friend recently told me "it is better to be just another fish in a healthy pond than the biggest fish in a dying pond." Another friend stated to me that "if you are the best teacher in your building, you are in the wrong building. You always want to be around people who make you better." I find both of these statements to be true and worth repeating often in education. When you are at an effective building, everyone wins, particularly the students. Each teacher feeds off the other and creates an atmosphere where it is a team effort to reach all students.

To hold on to your passion to affect the lives of students, you have to understand political rhetoric. Unfortunately, students lose when most politicians speak about education. They talk about reform before the last reform has even been implemented. Many say negative things about education and undermine the efforts by great teachers. They will leave an educator feeling gutted and angry. Most politicians never communicate with educators. It is important to remember the truth about education: your classroom and your school are what's important. Don't be swayed by opinions. Do your research. Know your field. Learn to spin a conversation when you hear negative talk about education. Family, friends and strangers at Walmart want to talk education when they are in your presence. You are an ambassador for education; keep the conversation positive. Focus on the students and the great impact teachers are having on the lives of those students. Get that person to talk about a teacher who inspired or encouraged him. Talk about how much you love the opportunity to fulfill your call. Protect your mind from the negative. Keep your eye on the prize. This does not mean that you shouldn't be active politically; it actually means the opposite. Every teacher should write their legislators and governor to let them know the great things that are happening every day in their classroom. You should inform them of school needs and pay attention to their voting record, but don't listen to the negative spew about the failures of education. The type of teacher who positively affects the lives of students is part of the solution, not the problem.

One thing that all effective teachers have in common is they know when they are done. Burnouts are not comfortable in an effective school. Every teacher has a season. Some people teach for five years as a season of their life, and some teach for forty. The important quality is that they are effective for the duration of their tenure. When an effective teacher realizes they have lost their passion, they bow out gracefully. I recently had a teacher inform me she was planning to retire at the end of the year. She wanted to inform me in November so I could quietly look for replacements. I attempted to talk her out of her decision. I let her know how she affected students every day. I told her how blessed her students were to have had the experience of her classroom. I even tried to alleviate any stress of the upcoming changes in curriculum, evaluations and an impending building move. She had close to thirty years in the position and she was uniquely talented. We talked, and I could tell she may be reconsidering her decision. She had blessed so many by her service. Then she looked me in the eye and said, "It's getting harder to get out of bed every day." I then realized her days were numbered. She no longer received the blessing. She was beginning to get excited about new chapters in her life. It is her time to bow out because she knew she would not be effective in the future if she continued. I also know there is someone else to take her place. I have learned in my position as an administrator to wait patiently for the right person. I will also admit to praying and networking to find the best people to teach in my building. It is that important.

So, if you are a middle school teacher, a college student considering the field, or a teacher from another grade level, middle school teachers come in all different packages. It is important that each teacher is in the right position, where they are effective to all students. They should be working side by side with a group of educators who have the same vision. Are you the type? Is there a type? What type of student will you reach?

PART TWO

THE EFFECTIVE CLASSROOM

SIX

STRUCTURED FREEDOM

When the middle school classroom is discussed, the first thing that comes to mind is student behavior. Nobody is thinking curriculum; they think, "How do I control a group of middle school students?" If a class is out of control, mayhem ensues and instruction cannot take place. Curriculum and objectives are an afterthought. Students must be under control in order for learning to occur. During my first year, my mentor looked at me and said, "Joey, it's called structured freedom."

When a middle school teacher can walk in to a classroom, speak a language that their students have been trained to understand, watch the students scurry across the room and get out materials, clean a workspace, and collaborate with one another like their paycheck depends on it, that teacher has established some solid procedures. Mrs. Deweese can begin the day by saying, "Please prepare for direct instruction." Forty-five students will stand up, move tables to one side of the room and gather with their binders by the whiteboard, prepared for any notes they would need to write down. Their chairs will be lined up and students are ready to learn. She could say, "Find a partner for pair share," and students would find a partner in the room within 15 seconds, sit down and quietly wait for her next instruction. The last couple of months of the school year, students will be scurrying around the room until they hear the bugle horn playing taps over the speaker. At that point, they all rush to line up on their side of the room. It is the Civil War simulation and they have to make sure they are at attention before their General, a student leader, comes to inspect their line and stance. Students actually self-monitor their procedures because they have work to complete. Occasionally, she can find a student to play an actual bugle instead of the recorded version. These are just a few of the procedures an amazing teacher taught her students in order to have a structured environment that gave freedom to the class. Students know the boundaries and are given tasks to complete. It's called structured freedom.

One of the greatest books on the shelves of educators is *The First Days of School* by Dr. Harry Wong. He did a great job of recognizing the best practices of educators and putting them all together for a structured environment. I give his book to all first year teachers in my building. The best middle school classrooms are those that have established procedures. In middle school, the students move toward conformity. They do not want to stick out as different in any way. In most cases, a parent or another teacher will let the principal know that a class is out of control. Students will rarely come to the principal and inform them of classroom problems, especially if the teacher has lost control of a class. Even good kids will generally not tell a principal if students are unruly. Once control has been lost, it is rare for a teacher to get it back.

During my tenure as a teacher at Thoreau Demonstration Academy, I witnessed a few teachers who could not handle a middle school classroom, but none stand out like the teacher across the hall my second year. The standards in this inner city school were set very high by a principal who knew how to get the best. It is a demonstration school, which means frequent visits by many professionals, some from very far away, expecting the execution of a perfect lesson. Thoreau is a high profile school that demands excellent teachers demonstrating multiple programs intended to work successfully. Tom Padalino was the first principal of this startup school that took 25% of their students by lottery from each side of town. When I was hired, I considered myself an excellent instructor and a blessing to any school that decided to employ me. After I met everyone and began my teaching career in this unique school, I realized I was just another teacher amongst many incredible instructors. Any place I had worked in the past, I was a rock star, but I was surrounded by rock stars in this building. I was challenged to differentiate the instruction and think outside of the box for assessments. I constantly felt like I was barely keeping my head above water by the challenge to teach in this building, but I was never challenged with keeping control of a class. Each time Mr. Padalino hired a new teacher, he would brag about his newfound treasure, telling every one of their history and accomplishments. He told us that Jeff was an adjunct college professor. He was alternatively certified and this was his first position in a public school. He left a lush office job making excellent money and his adjunct professorship for the public school classroom. He and a friend both took positions in high profile schools teaching math. I just knew he must be excellent if he could teach on the college level. He was a very nice person and had a nonchalant confidence toward his new profession. He didn't seem nervous; he was actually pretty laid back considering the challenge that awaited. We met regularly and discussed procedures and curriculum. As an 8th grade team, we would try to keep many procedures consistent in all core classes. Jeff would agree with the procedures during collaboration, and we would move forward. We even made matching posters to hang on the wall giving students a visual of all procedures.

Soon after the school year began, students told me he was "cool." He didn't make them raise their hand to talk. He had loose procedures for his classroom, and it wasn't long before I could hear the volume across the hall begin to rise. Eventually Mr. Padalino came to visit each member of the team, letting us know we needed to support Jeff. Jeff had gone to the office and informed them he had some problems with classroom behaviors. We attempted to talk with Jeff about his classroom management, offering supports, but he just nodded and said it was going to be okay. One day I saw him out in the hallway pacing. I came out to see what was happening. He told me that he had lost it with his students. He gave me some details of his language and a flying chair. He asked me if I had ever lost it like that. I told him I had allowed students to upset me before but never to that extent; I told him he was out of line. Jeff resigned before March of that school year. I later heard that his friend had resigned his teaching position about a month before Jeff. I seriously thought that if someone could teach college, they could teach middle school. I was wrong. In order to teach college, you must have mastery of the subject you are teaching. I have discovered that many people have adjunct teaching positions, with little skills in classroom control. College students choose to go to school and actually pay for the opportunity to sit in the classroom and glean brilliance from their professor. Middle school students are dragged there by their parents and dropped off with the hope and expectation they will listen to their teacher.

There isn't anything more difficult than keeping control of a group of middle school students, which is precisely why most people refuse the middle school environment. For those of us who have answered the call and chosen to embrace life in a middle school, it is essential we understand how to control a group of students. The key to controlling a group of students is a term called procedures, which are well-documented by Dr. Wong. Society says rules are meant to be broken, but procedures are meant to be followed. We have procedures for safety, such as walking in the halls and putting your backpack in your locker. We are able to talk in the hallway to our friends and freely choose to use the restroom and water fountains during our passing periods. I only mention the latter because it never fails sixth graders will ask me to use the restroom during our morning gathering time or lunch. Typically, elementary schools have very tight procedures. It takes them a little while to adjust to middle school and understand we don't need to know every time they go potty. These hallway procedures, when enforced by teachers standing in the halls, create a safe environment for everyone. We establish these procedures for the whole building during the first week of school. Students are brought to the auditorium and we review "what we do" rather than the two million things we should not do. Middle school students understand the reasoning behind the procedures. It is important to explain the purpose of the procedures. They are beginning to question everything at this point in their lives. They always want to know why they cannot do something or what the purpose is behind a procedure. We demonstrate in slow motion what can happen if they run in to someone full speed around a corner. Someone can get hurt. We explain the reasoning behind an adult greeting them at the door before they enter a room. First of all, we want to say hello to them every day. We also need to supervise them for safety reasons. They respect the answer when it makes sense.

Each teacher has her own procedures that she has developed with the rest of her team. Classroom teachers should have autonomy to develop their procedures, designed around their comfort level and personality, however it is essential that each teacher work with their team to develop common procedures so students have continuity in their classes. It might take a week to develop procedures in a classroom. Procedures need to be established and followed. It is so important that procedures are established during the first month of school that the leadership of our building is visiting each classroom and sending an instructional coach their direction at the first hint of a problem to help them re-establish procedures.

A quiet room isn't always the best environment. Some people believe a quiet classroom means it is a good teacher with control. I have to admit, as a teacher evaluator, I do like to walk in to a classroom and see that a teacher has control. A calm environment means that teacher must have scared them straight. But does a quiet environment mean that teacher is really good? Are all of the students learning? They could be doing an individual research project or they may be taking a quiz, but just because there is a quiet environment doesn't mean all students are learning. It may mean that they are scared, but fear does not mean they are learning. They may be reading a chapter and answering the questions at the end of the chapter for the hundredth time this year. A major misconception of an effective middle school classroom is that if it is quiet, it is effective. The best classrooms are active classrooms that seek to meet the learning styles of all students.

Active classrooms engage all students. I recently observed a classroom for the second time this school year. The ability of this teacher to involve all students in active learning is uncanny. I knew when I met her that she would be an amazing teacher. I literally recruited this teacher to teach at Madison because I knew she would be able to offer our students the most diversified learning experience afforded to middle school on a budget. I just thought it might take her a little longer to be teaching at this level. When I really think a teacher will be good in the interview process, I question whether I would be able to hold a candle to this teacher in a classroom. I hope that teachers are much better than I am because that means our students will benefit from the best. Although I recruited her to teach at my school, I am still surprised at her ability to reach all of her students. Mrs. Combs literally engages all of her students in each forty-five-minute class period. The students can hardly keep up with her, not because she is yelling or moving too quickly, but because she is constantly changing her approach. Multiple times during a short span, Mrs. Combs will ask the students to put something away and get something else out. She will challenge all seven learning styles in one setting.

In order to meet all of the learning styles and plan lessons that engage all students, you must have procedures in place that will keep all students safe and all lessons effective. A student must not impede other students from learning. That happens in the preparation of the procedures for the lesson. If the procedures are solid, very few students will ever be sent to the hall or office. Great teachers establish procedures for students during the first few weeks of school.

Once upon a time, in order to scare your students in to submission, you wouldn't smile till after Thanksgiving. It is true; this was a practice amongst teachers. It may not be written in books, but I heard this many times over from college to the classroom. I am sure that this was a scare tactic for the middle school above all others since they are the least forgiving. If you didn't smile, students did not know how to take you. You could be angry or sad, they were not sure, but it definitely kept them quiet for the first few months of school. In current times, if you do not smile, students will immediately think you are not a kind person. Students need to see you smile. They need to see smiles every day on the faces of their teachers. I am certain that a portion of our students do not see a smile every day unless it is on the face of a school employee. Teachers should show them how exciting it is to learn new concepts. Students should be greeted with a smile before entering each classroom every day. They should be dismissed by a smiling teacher each class period. Educators have to demonstrate to students that they belong in the classroom if they expect them to trust us. I once met a church youth worker named John Baumert. If you can imagine Sean Connery working with students, it is the most accurate description I can give of this unique individual. He was 64 years old and did not mind driving a bus 5 hours to church camp and leading a group of adolescents in Bible study twice a day. He would tell you he is old school, and he was right. I learned that John drove a bus for the local school system. John was a retired school shop teacher and really didn't need the money. He told me he drove a bus because students needed to be greeted with a smile when they jumped aboard the yellow bus each morning. After over 30 years of teaching, he knew the most important thing he could do in a day is make a student smile. Every classroom should have a teacher greeting students with a smile each hour. It is our first interaction with them for the class period and the best time to gauge their individual demeanors.

Appropriate classroom procedures have to be established in the first few weeks of school. If a teacher can cement and establish those procedures, more freedom can be experienced in the classroom. Middle school teachers can unfold these procedures and practice them as lessons demand. Students must be told the procedures before they get in trouble for not following them. It pains me to watch students not follow procedures the first few days of school, however, it is imperative that a teacher be patient as procedures are established. It should be explained specifically to the whole class when a new procedure is implemented. Each student's attention should be dedicated to the teacher, meaning that the teacher can see every eye in the room. After a procedure has been explained and practiced, the students are responsible for following the procedure.

It is very important to understand the teacher is responsible for holding students accountable for following the procedures. In the classrooms that get out of control, it is more often because the teacher is allowing the students to work outside of the procedures. When middle school students realize that you are not serious about procedures, they will test every boundary you have set. Do you remember the movie *Jurassic Park*? There is a part of the movie where the T-Rex is hitting the electric fence and shocking himself. It was implied that maybe the dinosaur wasn't very bright because that must have hurt. Then in a calm voice the actor reveals, "He is checking for weak spots in the fence." If the dinosaur finds a weak spot, he can break through the fence. Middle school students are much like a T-Rex, they will test your boundaries. If you have set procedures or boundaries for students and a student tests the boundaries, you must address that immediately. It isn't just the tough students that test boundaries, most students will test boundaries. When a student blurts out an answer, they need to be reminded to raise their hand. If a student gets up to sharpen their pencil during direct instruction, the teacher needs to ask them, "When is the appropriate time to sharpen your pencil?" Most students will answer the question and follow procedures in the future. If a teacher does not address the problem, other students will read that as an opportunity to ignore procedures in the future. If a teacher asks for the attention of the class, they must wait until all students are quiet before addressing the class. When a teacher begins to talk over the students, they have nonverbally told the students that they do not have to listen.

If a teacher has established a set of procedures, the classroom becomes a fertile ground for young minds to flourish. Students understand the boundaries, and the classroom is a safe place to learn. Lesson planning becomes much easier because you know what to expect from each hour. You have a handle on the class. When you talk to a veteran teacher, they will inevitably let you know how far along a class has come in their ability to understand and follow procedures. When I speak of veteran teachers, I mean the seasoned professionals who love working in middle school. The educators who have established procedures for decades and are still excited about coming to work every day.

Veteran teachers are great resources for developing procedures. New teachers should seek out any veteran teachers and find out what has worked for them. How do they set up procedures and what mistakes have they made? A common misconception is that schools need constant reform (or a new group of teachers), and we "throw the baby out with the bathwater." I used that old saying last month with my assistant principal about a program we were discussing and he said I sounded like his father, using statements he doesn't understand. Prior to indoor plumbing (and many other sanitary measures), families used to fill a bathtub with water once a month and start with the father and mother taking their baths first. Without changing the water, each child from oldest to youngest would bathe. By the time it was the last child, usually a baby, you could lose the child in the water because it was so dirty. Hence the saying, *don't throw the baby out with the bathwater*. Just like aphoristic statements from previous generations, there are valuable lessons to learn from seasoned teachers. They can connect generations and prepare growing teachers. Although there are amazing teachers right out of college, seasoned teachers can bring a calmness to any situation because they have experienced most challenges. When a teacher dedicates over 20 years of his life to middle school students, approaches each day with enthusiasm, and still has a desire to learn new skills, it is imperative that we cultivate every opportunity for them to interact with new, growing teachers.

Once you have established your procedures, a middle school class will be a safe environment for all students to learn. Students will understand what is expected of them for independent learning time, pair share, or they can get in a learning group of any size. The teacher will have the freedom to set up her class to meet the learning needs of all students. You can have reading time set up where some students are reading independently, some are in pairs or groups, and some are with you. You have established a level of freedom to learn in your classroom. Students know when to raise their hands, when they can use the restroom and the appropriate time to sharpen their pencil. Interruptions are minimal because students know their responsibility in the classroom. You can also look in the mirror and know that you have gone where only a few educators have the ability to go. You are not just surviving middle school at this point, *you are beginning to thrive*. Very few people can go beyond scaring a group of middle school students to keep control, and most individuals could not even go that far. Although it is not rocket science, it might as well be to the normal individual. One thing is very certain-it takes a special person to manage a classroom full of middle school students. Structured freedom, when established, allows all students to meet their maximum potential.

Do you have the rare ability to control a group of early adolescents? Does a safe and active learning environment come naturally for you? Can you competently set boundaries for students?

SEVEN

BEST PRACTICES

The best practices in a middle school classroom have been tested and refined over generations. It is important to embrace the lessons of the past when planning for the future. There is always something new to be discovered, but it is much easier and effective to refine someone else's practices than to reinvent the wheel every day.

The most effective classrooms have a high level of student engagement. It is obvious when you open the door if students are actively learning. I work with a science teacher who keeps students engaged every day. Mrs. Miller will try to have her students complete as many science labs in a year as possible, because she understands the importance of student engagement. She knows if she can put their hands on manipulatives, her students are more likely to remember the content. When students are working on labs, they have to answer several questions, which will cause their brain to process what they have learned. Whether it is a lab, a daily question, an inquiry or a project, Mrs. Miller's room is engaging every day. When classrooms are engaged, the students are learning. I have seen many engaging classrooms, where the students' complete thought process is consumed with curriculum, instead of their phone under the table. The greatest responsibility for our teachers is to engage their students through exciting lessons.

When students are engaged in curriculum, they are typically not having behavioral problems. When students are busy working, they don't have the time or opportunity to get in to trouble. When their brains are thinking about the positive things that are happening and learning is taking place, they do not get bored. Most students get in to trouble because they are bored. It is okay for a student to feel overwhelmed, confused or excited about the classroom expectations. If a student is bored, it is time to rethink the lesson plans. Keeping all students engaged is all about planning. When you have accounted for all variables in a lesson, you have considered what each child needs in order to stay engaged. When a lesson is well planned, execution is simple

Effective classrooms make every day count. It baffles me to think why we would force a group of young people to come to school, pay for very expensive facilities, and hire highly qualified instructors to have a free day of class. I have heard of these free days and party days, but never witnessed them in person as a professional (my principal wouldn't allow them and I will not allow them either). I cannot imagine why anyone would want to go to school for four years, take grueling tests to become highly qualified to teach and work for pennies, so they can take days off and let students do nothing in a classroom. What a wasted opportunity. The message we give students is that their time is not valuable. Students will take the curriculum seriously when we take their time seriously. The time of our students is valuable. Every teacher should let his students know how valuable their time is to them. Each day should be filled with opportunities to experience learning.

Anytime there is a party in class, it should relate to the curriculum. Students love to laugh and have fun, but there must be a purpose. There are movies shown every day in classrooms that have no relation to curriculum. It is okay to watch a movie in a classroom, after you have read the book or to emphasize or enhance the curriculum. Maybe you are showing a movie clip, so students can get a glimpse of the culture or dress from a period. That would be appropriate. Just watching a comedy in a classroom has not only wasted valuable moments in student learning but has damaged the reputation of the profession. In the schools I have been an educator, parties and movies have been tied to the curriculum. Students should be able to tell a visitor exactly what they are learning in any lesson. They should know that their time is valued by every adult in the building. When we model that to them, they will take their own time seriously.

Effective classrooms are curriculum rich and challenging. Although it sounds like a no-brainer, students should know what they are learning. They should be able to look on the board or a wall and show you a short-term learning objective. They should be able to see the agenda covering their week. Walls and bulletin boards should teach. All visible items in a room serve a purpose to instruct our students. Students will not question the difficulty because the rigor will always sufficiently challenge them. A visitor should walk in and be able to figure out what the students are learning by observation. Students in an effective classroom will tell a visitor what they are working on and what they are learning.

Curriculum should be integrated. A student is more likely to remember a concept if it is integrated with other subjects. This involves high levels of communication between teachers on a team. When students know they will be using a writing technique in their science class, it solidifies what they have learned in English. As a teacher, our science and math teachers would consistently use four square writing because that was the prewrite method we would teach our students. They knew when we would begin our concentration on writing essays and integrate the curriculum. When the students wrote a report in science, they used the same writing method as their English teacher taught. The students heard the same language in every core class. Eventually, even the elective teachers were integrating the writing methods because it was effective. I personally taught English and History integrated. Although it is initially a challenge to overcome the paradigm of separating curriculum, the benefit of students connecting the two subjects was invaluable. Most of the time, students didn't even notice the difference between subjects. When we read a novel, many times it was historical fiction. Many of their writing assignments were integrated with history inquiries. Students only received one grade in the class because the subjects were integrated and impossible to separate. We also met weekly with the science and math teachers to integrate subjects, which resulted in the students making connections across all curriculum. My current school district has the disciplines traditionally divided by class period. Each teaching team uses their team plan to integrate curriculum effectively.

Curriculum should challenge all intelligence levels. Teachers in the most effective classrooms challenge all of their students. We have failed a student if they get bored. If a student gets bored, most of the time it is a highly intelligent student. There should be a level of rigor in the curriculum encouraging all students to achieve at a high level. Each child should encounter a level of rigor to cause them to struggle. From the struggle comes the learning. When students struggle, they also develop a work ethic. If a student did not struggle in middle school, what will be his resolve when he begins to struggle in high school or college? If a student gives up because she doesn't understand, we find them more supports. Effective teachers will unabashedly tell students they expect them to be successful. They will always have high expectations for their students.

An effective classroom has an enthusiastic instructor who sees teaching as a privilege. Everyone remembers his favorite class. Someone who is enthusiastic about what she teaches usually teaches that favorite class. It is hard to fake enthusiasm. A great teacher can look over lesson plans and follow them. They can even reach a group of students who are self-starters and just need some direction. But a teacher who wants the majority of his students to dig deeply into the content needs to be interested in the concepts he is teaching.

Dr. Thompson was my college freshman history teacher. I took his class because another student said he was great, and his class was packed with familiar faces. He brought a guitar one day to a college class and sang us a song about the life of a common man during the industrial revolution. When he spoke about history, he wanted us to understand the time period. He told us a story about meeting Harry Truman. He was an 8th grade student, growing up in Missouri in the mid 1950's. Despite the discouragement from his teacher and parents, he wrote the former President, as part of a class project to do a career shadow day. To everyone's surprise, President Truman personally wrote him back and he shadowed him for a morning. He spent a class period telling us about a half day of his life four decades ago. Not one person moved; we were mesmerized by the genuine respect he had for the President. He probably told that story hundreds of times, if not more. It was as if he was sharing it for the first time. He loved history, and so did we because we had Dr. Thompson. I enjoyed his class so much, I took two more courses from him that did not count in my degree plan. Harry Truman immediately became one of my favorite Presidents. Dr. Thompson's love for his content spilled on me, and I began to have passion and love the subject as he did.

Every great teacher has a level of humility because they know they are privileged to have the honor to instruct. Although some level of arrogance is inevitable, tolerated, and expected with highly intelligent people, teachers know they get to do what they love for a living. They will treat the class with true appreciation for the gift of their precious time. Most teachers cannot help but get emotional for the true honor it is to stand before a group of students and be responsible for their learning. That emotion could be tears of joy or pain, depending on whether they are in the right place.

Great classrooms are safe for all students. It is extremely important that every student feels safe in each classroom.

Although we make physical safety the biggest priority in schools, students have to feel safe in a classroom to give their personal best. They need to feel safe socially and emotionally, just like they feel safe physically. It is the responsibility of the teacher to make this happen. The teacher is the leader and sets the tone of how students will treat each other. Middle school students turn in to introverts because they are conforming to the group. They hate to stick out and the slightest giggle will cause anxiety. Students need to feel safe to speak up and share in a class. Students need to feel safe in order to perform in front of the class, when a lesson affords the opportunity for their learning style. Procedures must be explained, practiced and enforced that enable students to take risks without risking ridicule. Teachers also lead the way to celebrate student success. Students must be allowed to ask questions freely, receiving clear answers. Students need the opportunity to share freely, especially when they have an opinion about the subject. When a middle school student is discussing *The Outsiders* in class, he must be able to share his true feelings about a character in order to relate to the book and the author. *To Kill a Mockingbird* is a staple in schools across America. Students must be able to openly share emotions of fear and anger about the story. In every class the students attend, they need to feel safe to learn.

Great classrooms have a real world connection. Most students will eventually ask you what this has to do with their life. When will they ever use this? Why do they need to learn this? Great teachers understand they have to connect their content to the real world. Teachers who understand this importance make it look easy. They have been connecting it for themselves. English teachers have their students write resumes and thank you letters. They have them connecting to the character of a book. Math teachers inevitably are peppered with questions of purpose more any other subject. They will connect their lesson with money, cars and shopping. Every word problem from a math teacher will relate to their students' lives. History teachers have their students dress up and reenact an event in history. They don't just read about the Underground Railroad; they relive the Underground Railroad. They will play videos that relate to the time period. They will take whatever measure needed to make the subject come alive. Science teachers give the students all of the hands-on experience possible because they know the students will remember observing the chemical reaction better than by just reading about it. Great teachers bring in guests to share their experience. There is no better connection to the real world than actually taking the students to see the real world. If the opportunity is available, the best practice for any educator is to give their students real life experience.

The effective classroom consistently seeks to meet the learning style of all students. I was given an assignment in middle school to read a chapter for understanding. I had to be prepared to answer questions from the teacher. Although I read the chapter of the book multiple times, I still could not retain the information. I remember telling my mom that she can expect a lower grade for this class because I couldn't understand anything I was reading. She then told me a story about her learning style. She told me that she had to go to the back room of the small house where she grew up, shut the door, and read out loud. She said when she read silently, she didn't retain the information, but when she read out loud to herself, she could remember what she read. She told me I should try that method to see if it would help me retain knowledge. I had never heard of the concept. I took my book to our back bedroom, where my brother was least likely to hear me and ridicule me, and I read out loud. I remembered what I read. I learned I was an auditory learner before I had ever heard of learning styles. Because of this discovery, I know that if I am not particularly interested in a book I need to read, I have to go read it out loud. When I get a moment alone, which is quite rare, I read everything aloud. While it is a shame it took so long to understand learning styles and differentiated instruction, it is a blessing to know we can reach our students through multiple channels. Auditory is not my only learning style, I am also very kinesthetic and visual. Most people favor multiple learning styles. With each learning style, we are using different areas of our brain. The most effective classrooms give students options that allow them to choose their learning style. They also expose students to every learning style, so students are able to experience and respect others modes of learning. Each student also needs to use all areas of their brain. During middle school, many students' learning styles change because they are changing. Effective classrooms intentionally prepare to cover all learning styles with their students. Each unit, every concept may be learned through differentiated lessons. Effective educators spend more time in the planning phase of lesson plans and spend less energy administering the lesson. It is much harder to plan a lesson that reaches all students than to execute the lesson. You will actually have fun during a lesson watching it unfold. You find yourself excited for certain students because you know the light bulb will go off in their heads and they will begin to understand the concepts.

Effective classrooms do not make it easy for a student to fail. We have all heard of the programs and mottos. Failure isn't an option and zeroes are not permitted are a couple of them. We even have great acronyms for the programs. Not allowing student failures cannot be a policy in middle school. It has to be a philosophy. If we just say we are not allowing failing grades, students will catch on quickly, especially in middle school. They will take advantage of the great new option of exerting the least amount of energy and still passing the class. This is the equivalent of me blowing off my mandatory book study after school in lieu of a good afternoon of fishing and still collecting a paycheck. That is a no brainer: I am going fishing. My sister-in-law was a teacher in an elementary school where they were not allowed to fail any students. The students knew you could not hold them accountable and they paid disastrous consequences. The students were not only sliding by but were being cheated of knowledge they should have been expected to retain. She experienced burnout quickly and decided to move to a district with a different philosophy. Effective schools have an option to keep students in from lunch or elective classes to remediate. Most of the time this will work. Students definitely want their social time in middle school. Most of them love their elective classes and consider it cruel and unusual punishment to rob them of that time. However, there are students who will purposefully not complete their work and depend on a teacher to make the effort to remove them from lunch or another class. They noticeably feed off the special attention given to them. Effective educators know they have been hired for one purpose, student learning. If a student makes it through their class and does not learn, the teacher feels like she has failed.

The philosophy should be failure is not an option. This is the philosophy of effective educators who give students every opportunity to learn. Teachers take it personally when students are not learning the objectives they teach. They see their mission as incomplete unless they are reaching every student. Some students have mental and emotional issues that adversely affect their learning opportunities. Most students who are failing after all remedial efforts have proven ineffective have issues beyond the scope of learning styles. Sometimes the issues go beyond the skillset of the teacher. Even a meeting with a parent or guardian doesn't always produce the results we would like. Most parents are at a loss by this point. These students have opportunities for school counseling and outside counseling. Effective educators learn of these issues early and get help for their students. They make every effort to ensure each student learns the objectives and are prepared for the challenges of the next grade level. If a student fails, it is because they forced themselves through the cracks. Effective educators give them every option. They use every trick and afford every opportunity to get students to learn. If a student did not learn, it wasn't because of a lack of effort from a teacher.

Teachers in effective middle school classrooms will have all students participate in a learning group. Groups should be integrated by culture, gender and ability. Some teachers keep them in their learning group at all times, particularly if they have tables instead of desks. Some teachers leave their desks grouped together. Groups will have procedures and rubrics with every assignment. Students should ask two members of their learning group before approaching the teacher with a question. During group projects, students will fill out a rubric to document the level of work each student completed. When you mix ability levels, struggling students will perform better than if given the assignment and left by themselves. Higher performing students will continue to perform at a high level while assisting struggling students. Learning groups encourage a level of teamwork as well as teaching them valuable character traits such as listening, mutual respect, and perseverance.

An effective classroom uses technology. Technology is a constantly changing force in today's society, and it should affect the classroom. I dare not even reference a form of technology for fear this book will be obsolete and a laughingstock before it is published. As new technology is introduced and schools are able to use new forms, it is critical they adapt to this ever-changing world. It is also err to believe technology will do all of the work to properly instruct our students. We are cheating our students if we believe they can look at a screen of any kind solely for their source of instruction. The last decade has shown us what technology at our fingertips can provide. We can research information and reference a video in a snap. Books have disappeared from libraries in lieu of digital formats. Music is easier to access. It is important to embrace any technology that enhances the learning environment as a supplement to lessons that meet every learning style. You will never impress a student with the use of technology in your lesson. Once upon a time, school technology surpassed the technology at home. The slide projector and 8mm movies were incredible tools of yesteryear. The overhead projector replaced all that daily writing on the chalkboard. Not only were they useful tools, but they were also very entertaining. The phones and apps they have downloaded are their entertainment today. Every teacher should model what technology can do for you professionally. Teachers should be putting any available technology in the hands of their students because they will inevitably need it for their future. Effective classrooms utilize all tools at their disposal and draw upon a broad repertoire of knowledge to reach students. Middle school students will try to hide if you let them. Great teachers will not let a student hide behind technology, but rather show their students how to use technology to enhance their learning.

Effective classrooms are friendly and inviting to outside guests. In effective learning environments, students will invite visitors to become part of the lesson. Students will recognize when a visitor walks in and introduce themselves. They will invite the outside visitor to their learning group and introduce them to each member. Effective teachers set a positive tone for guests who enter their classroom. They make sure students speak in complete sentences. They encourage students to greet guests. Students see it as a privilege. The students are polite because the teacher is polite. Students love to share what they are learning. After a few minutes, they forget there is an adult in their presence and just treat them as a peer. Students are more open in their learning groups than they will be in the hallway or at lunchtime. They enjoy when you meet them in their world.

Effective middle school classrooms have an active environment. All classrooms should be active. Middle school students need physical stimulation. It is ideal for them to be able to move around when learning. Effective classrooms consistently provide opportunities for students to learn in an active environment created by teachers who value student learning. I cannot imagine an effective classroom in middle school that is not active. It is imperative that students are able to move, especially in middle school. It is a great feat to harness their energy for learning experiences. Middle school students are waiting for the opportunity to jump up and do something. Whenever I would look at my class and say "when I say get up, this is what you are going to do", there would be an incredible look of excitement in their eyes. They just knew the class period was going to be a blast. They would listen intently because they understood directions must be followed or risk an alternative lesson plan, which wasn't active. As an administrator, I often ask students their opinion of a class. They will inevitably tell me if it is an active classroom. They don't specify what they are doing that day, they will tell me something they did the week before. They will tell me of the time they were given a task and expected to inquire and present or a multitude of other active assignments. Whether there be a simulation or a practice game, active classrooms provide excitement to the learning experience that students will not forget. It is important to note that active rooms do not necessarily mean noisy. I have witnessed poetry tours and underground railroad simulations that you could hear a pin drop, but they were still very active and produced amazing retention.

Have you experienced an effective classroom? Is your classroom effective? Are your students engaged in a curriculum rich environment? Do students feel safe to contribute? Is the environment friendly and inviting? Do students make a real world connection? Have you done everything possible to keep a child from falling through the cracks? Although an accurate list does not exist for every practice, these are essential to master before you have an effective classroom. Every middle school child deserves a schedule with all highly effective classrooms.

EIGHT

THE PARENT

To completely reach every student and have an effective classroom approach, you must involve the middle school parent. The effective educator seeks to understand the parent.

I have heard from youth workers from multiple professions who wish they could just deal with the student and eliminate the parent. They say if we could just deal with the students, and not have the parent in the equation, that would make life easy. There is truth to the statement, but if we did not involve the parents, we would never be able to completely reach the child. If you are called to work in middle school, handling a group of students eventually becomes second nature. Parents are an extremely important part of the process when educating the students because they are the ultimate authority over the child. The educator and parent must work together to have the most effective approach to educating children. Parents hold the students accountable for what they are responsible to complete at home. If the parent is not supportive of the classroom efforts, the student is not accountable when they go home. The question is, how do we get the parent involved to support the classroom? A parent will benefit personally as much from a healthy relationship as the educator.

The parent should be the students strongest advocate. Every student deserves a person who will be in their corner and look after their best interests. They should protect them from dangers and make sure they are challenged academically. They love their children and want to see them grow in to contributing members of society. I have seen parents that have been amazing advocates for their child and I have seen children without an advocate. I once had a student in the foster system who was a frequent visitor to the office. When I would call the foster mom to inform her of a particular incident and the discipline that would follow, she would ask for more discipline. She wanted it to be harsher. I felt as if I needed to be the advocate for the student because a strong parental figure will discipline at home but never depend on the school to be their strong arm. Most sensible parents advocate for their children by giving them their best wisdom in making decisions and let them live with consequences. Parents want their children to do well in school and every effective educator wants their partnership.

The parent advocate can take on a couple of different roles, depending on the actions of the educator. The parent can be a supportive partner, who reinforces academics and behavior, because they have an understanding and trust of the teacher. The parent does not get sidelined or distracted by student claims of over reaching rigorous expectations, lost papers, or teacher favorites. The circle of accountability becomes complete and the student has no place to fall through a crack. The parent can take on the role of the skeptical student advocate who questions the teacher's every move. When there is a group of parents taking on the latter role, or anywhere in between, it becomes more difficult for the teacher to accomplish her goals. Students will inevitably try to get out of rigor when it means they have to work, especially middle school students. Middle school students will be lazy if they are not held accountable. Middle school students will not only fall through the cracks if you allow them, they will walk through the cracks they create with a wedge between the parent and teacher. For this reason, it is vital to have a working relationship with all parents.

You must make the parent your ally. The parent has to understand that you are working together in the best interest of the student. Parents need to be our partners. We have the same goals and desires, which is for their child to be successful. Many times this concept is lost. Parents will quickly be the defender of their child. Many of them are defensive before they meet you. Educators must strategize to make the parent an ally as quickly as possible. When we have an ally in the parent, we have a full circle support system for the student.

In order to make the parent your ally, you must first seek to understand the parent. Each student comes from a different family. Schools are a microcosm of society. There is no longer a normal when it comes to family dynamics. At one time, there was a typical family dynamic to which everyone was accustomed. Although that is no longer the case, most students still have a parent to whom they are responsible. Sometimes there are two. More often than not, teachers will experience parents, step parents and grandparents in any given classroom. I recently led a meeting with one biological parent and two step parents. Sometimes the lead parent switches off mid year. I currently have a student living with her father's girlfriend because her dad is serving a short prison sentence. I remember when she lived with her mom. We have spoken to four different guardians for her and she is still doing well, despite her situation. Regardless of the family dynamic, the student is the focus. The goal in the whole situation is to make sure the student is successful through educators working with parents. To best understand the middle school parent, you must understand they are suddenly being treated differently at home by the student, they have anxiety about their past experience of junior high/middle school, they are giving you their best, and communication is always key.

It is also important to note that some parents are going

through all of this with their child. For many of us, our parents were observers. For our more fortunate children, parents are in daily communication with their child and nothing is hitting them by complete surprise. Teachers will encounter both ends of the spectrum with parents. The parents who are in daily communication with their children have a better relationship and will experience much more joy in their child's middle years. They embrace the challenges they will face and guide their child each step of the way. Other parents are being hit completely by surprise at every turn for a variety of reasons. More often than not, the children with involved parents have an easier road ahead of them and middle school is a joyous adventure.

Every parent is experiencing a difference in their child at home. Each child has differing characteristics and they all develop at different rates. Although there are numerous variables, there are some constants in middle school. They will all hit puberty. They will grow rapidly. They are much more emotional. Their friends many times change and become much more important, usually surpassing the family. They become interested in the opposite sex. Their interests begin to change as well as their habits. These characteristics create a roller coaster for the parents as well, because they are being treated differently by their child.

As much as every parent believes they are prepared for puberty, there are always surprises. The students are doubling in size and there are growing pains for the parents. Puberty is usually accompanied by emotional swings. As discussed previously, the amount of hormone going though the adolescent body is like a drug. The fact that they get moody and have an attitude is not surprising, when you put it all in to context. It is still not easy on the parents. It is as if it hit them by surprise. Their baby, who has always been respectful has recently acquired an opinion accompanied by an attitude. Most parents have had 11 years of even-keeled emotions comparative to what they are experiencing. They know their child very well. Their child is very concrete in their thinking.

Many parents come to middle school very confident they are ready for the puberty phase because they have been through it, remember the problems they had, and will not let their child make the same mistakes they made. Nothing will surprise them. They will tell their child what to do and save them from the insecurity and frustration. They will prepare their child and they will not tolerate an attitude. This will not be difficult because they have it mastered in their mind. No parent can properly prepare for their child going through puberty. There has never been a parent who has made it through the middle years without a bump in the road, more likely a few craters. Most parents have wondered if they know their child. They usually hit their limit of attitude before 7th grade is complete. As they develop through puberty, their friendships can change multiple times.

Parents typically have become accustomed to a childhood best friend from elementary. They have probably even gotten to know their parents very well. Their best friend is like one of the family. They have been on vacations and family gatherings. They have gotten to know the parents of their friend and trust their children at their friend's home. Suddenly there are new people in their life. Their child is now talking about different friends. If allowed, they're even bringing home new friends. The parents are in a tailspin, wondering if this is the best thing for their children. Students might even change their circle of friends multiple times, furthering the stress of their parents. Their friends take on the role of family.

Friends become more important than family. Students want to spend more time with their friends in middle school. They are confiding in their friends and their parents are being shut out of their life. Parents who could easily get their child to speak to them have suddenly found themselves forcing the conversation. Just to get the normal information from their day has become a major task. Most students will go through a phase where they do not want to be seen with their parents. I recently had a very supportive parent pull through the front drive of the school to drop off her child. I said hello to the child as he walked by and waved at the parent, still in her car. She shook her head in disgust and pulled up to the visitors' parking about four cars away. I was concerned as I have only seen this parent smile in the past. She is a model of support and extremely kind. As she walked by she let me know her son did not want her to walk in the school with him. She needed to put money in his lunch account. He would have preferred not to be seen with her, even for just a walk down the hallway. It is as if the students do not want their friends to know they have a family. With social media, they can stay plugged in to their friends at all times.

As if the parent isn't already feeling a little shut out and out of touch, the middle school student starts becoming much more interested in the opposite sex. The very quiet phone conversations, holding hands walking down the hallway, and that awkward ride to the movies is a reality experienced by the majority of parents. Almost every student can recall their first "real" crush during middle school. This is where many learn about relationships, either their own or their friends.

They are bringing home different friends, talking to the opposite sex, growing by the minute, eating everything in the fridge, and they are emotional and moody. The middle school parent has suddenly realized that they are in the twilight zone. They're confused, frustrated, and scared. If we are to understand the parent, we must comprehend they are seeing a different child at home.

Every parent has different emerging emotions as they walk onto the campus of a middle school. Many of them have a genuine anxiety. Some emotions surface because of the way they feel about their child, some of them emerge because of the way they feel about their junior high/middle school experience. If a parent went to middle school at Madison, they will inevitably tell me about their experience as they walk back down the hallway, recalling teachers and friends. Almost every disciplinary meeting includes the parents' middle school experience as part of the conversation. I recently witnessed a man approaching the school. He looked angry and he was very puffed up like he was looking for a confrontation. I leaned over to my assistant principal and stated that I hoped he was looking for him and not me. As he got closer to the school, I realized he was much bigger than me and I had better diffuse the situation before he gets near any children or adults in which he might have a problem. When I said hello, he immediately erased the scowl from his face and took a breath. He said hello and I directed him where he could drop off some papers. He wasn't angry at any current situation, but you could tell he had anxiety about walking into a school.

Some parents have bad memories of middle school and some have great memories. I have been very fortunate to have had the same individual lead our parent support group for the majority of my tenure as principal. She has taken the role because she had a great middle school experience at Madison. She wanted to create a wonderful experience for both of her sons. She considers middle school her best years.

Most parents have already concluded what subjects are interesting and useful, or which are boring and useless, because of the teachers that have affected their life in middle school. When I taught middle school, many parents would approach me at back to school night, a few weeks into the first semester, excited for their child. They had a boring history teacher when they were in middle school, and they were very complimentary of my abilities to connect their children to the content. Many parents just assumed that I was hired to coach because I taught history and were surprised when their child came home excited about my class. They would thank me for making the subject come alive for their child.

I hear wonderful stories from parents of the impact that teachers, sports, and activities had on their life. I also hear horror stories from parents about how they feel about middle school from their experience. No matter where the parents are coming from, the most important thing in their lives is coming your way. It is the educators job to make them understand they have their students best interest at heart. When they walk onto that campus, they are still feeling their emotions of middle school until we make them feel differently.

My former principal used to comment on a consistent basis that parents are sending us their best. She would also say that we only have their child for a few years, but the parents have them for a lifetime. Both statements ring very true, for the well-behaved studious kids and the challenging kids. The parents are sending us their precious best, and they know they will be living with them for a lifetime. The parents are not holding out on us. There isn't a more disciplined or respectful child they have been waiting to send. They aren't hiding a student that is more driven or has a higher IQ. This is their best. They know this is their one chance and we are there to help them. The best way we can help parents is through communication.

Communication is the key to any relationship. We live in a world of constant interaction. If there is one thing that has changed in the last couple of decades, it is our ability to communicate more efficiently. People expect to know things instantaneously. We used to give out progress reports in the middle of a quarter. A parent would not know their child was flunking until five weeks in to the semester. Now we have grades posted online. Parents can check their students grades at any time. Some parents check daily. They can also check on each assignment. There are parents who will anticipate instant grading. At one time, parents didn't know their child was in trouble until the principal called. It is rare that a parent hasn't been informed by their child or by one of their friends if they are in the office. Parents are accustomed to instant communication. Parents expect a level of communication regarding their child and effective educators continue to be innovative in their approaches to inform parents.

Understanding what is happening with the parent at home is an important first step. The next step is to understand what the parents need to know in order to trust the teacher. In order to make a parent your ally, they need to hear that you like their child, you are aware of their child's learning styles, you will challenge their child, and their student is learning in your class.

One of the most important things you can do is to let a parent know that you like their child. If they know you like their child, you will have their support in most situations. More often than not, it is the student that will let the parent know if they feel they are liked by the teacher. Unfortunately, you will not have a chance to interact with every parent because they are too busy, unless there is a problem. When there is a problem, one of the first things a parent needs to hear from the teacher is that their child has some redeeming quality that you can identify, before they hear of behavior problems or academic issues. Most parents are initially defensive when they come to a meeting to discuss their child's behavior or academics. You can tell by their posture and tones. I recently greeted a set of parents in the front office and brought them to a conference room. When I greeted them, the father didn't even speak. He just nodded without expression as I said hello. Once in the meeting, each teacher, counselor, and administrator spoke about the child's behavior. All started the conversation with a specific compliment of the student before discussing the problems in the classroom. By the end of the meeting, both parents were relaxed and comfortable with every person, because they realized the teaching team and administration liked their child. The father stood up and approached me to shake hands before he left. If a parent does not hear from the student or the teacher that their child is cared about, you will not have a parent ally.

Every parent needs to know that you are meeting their child's learning style. It is not acceptable to recycle the same approach to a lesson every day. A teacher must differentiate the instruction based upon his students learning styles. An effective teacher presents the objectives multiple ways each day. He is aware of the brain research and how important it is for each child to be presented curriculum in different modes to meet their learning styles. A teacher should be able to identify a learning style to parents. The teacher is the expert in the classroom and the parents are looking for that expertise when educating their child. When a student comes home and expresses that a teacher has presented the information so that their child can comprehend, there is a newfound trust in the teacher.

Parents need to know every teacher will challenge their child each day in the classroom. Every parent appreciates accolades about their children. They are proud when their child makes a good grade in a class. The parents also expect a level of rigor in the curriculum. Some students can learn quickly and get bored. Some students need extra help. No matter the level, all students need to be challenged. The responsibility is on the teacher to plan the lessons to challenge each child. It is a colossal waste of time for a student to come to school and not be challenged. No child should ever be bored in a classroom. It is a disservice to the student to make them the teacher's helper because they comprehend too quickly. Every child should experience a rigor to the curriculum that matches their individual ability. When a child struggles, but still experiences success, the parent knows that the teacher has successfully challenged their child academically. Students will always walk away from a rigorous class appreciative because of what they learned.

Nothing excites a parent more about the classroom than their child's enthusiasm for learning. When you have broken the barriers of familial silence because the student cannot contain their excitement from the day's acquired knowledge, the parents will know their child is learning and have an appreciation for the teacher. The child will talk before the parents ask the question, "How was your day?" They will tell of their new found knowledge and what they discovered for the day. They may even be the ones asking the question of the parents. Parents would prefer that their child come home daily with newfound knowledge and excitement than a test score. Every parent wants to know their child is learning. Every parent appreciates a teacher who shows their child a love for learning.

When an educator seeks to understand the parent,

and the parent sees the evidence their child is cared for and learning at school, the most important partnership for the benefit of the child is formed. The entire goal is to involve the parent in the student's education. The parent will be the ally of the teacher and a level of involvement will inevitably be available.

When it comes to the involvement of parents, the classroom teacher has a much better opportunity to involve the parent than the school. Most parents would prefer to be involved in the daily classroom life than any school activity or function. There are countless parent volunteers who never darken the door of the office. I have seen parents who have a disdain for school in general, come to school dressed up in character for a particular class. Teachers can connect to parents when the administration cannot.

When teachers can connect with the parent and make them their ally, it is also very beneficial for the parent. They can glean from the teacher's wisdom. Teachers live in the world of students. They know their age group and get to know their students individually. The parent only has one child this age. They do not live in the world of adolescents and they do not understand what is happening. Effective teachers keep an open line of communication with parents. Parents can email or call a teacher to find out if their child is hanging around the right students.

If a teacher has developed a rapport with the student, many times the student will seek the advice of the teacher before their parents. Students are looking for direction and the parent's opinion loses credibility at this age. More often than not, the teacher gives the exact same advice that the parent will give. The parent-teacher ally becomes even more important to the parents when they know their student will get appropriate direction from the teacher.

If a teacher knows this age group and has a good rapport with the students, their expertise is invaluable to the parents. As needs arise, I have kept a constant stream of opportunities for students to volunteer their services after school. Inevitably, it has allowed me the chance to develop relationships and teach students how to paint, stain or build. When students are with their friends or in small groups, they will forget that an adult is in their presence and they begin openly talking. I will generally get an insight for that group of students. They will usually ask what I think or eventually involve me in their conversation. Every single year, a parent of one those students contacts me to ask my advice on what to do in a situation with their child. Sometimes they will ask me to speak to their child. Sometimes they will just ask to keep the conversation confidential. They just need to hear exactly what is going on with their child and their behavior is normal. They need to hear that their child will be okay. Educators have a huge opportunity to effect the lives of students as a trusted confidant. That window of opportunity is very short but absolutely paramount. Teachers should be a huge resource for the parent. This only serves the students best interest when the parents and teachers have a good relationship.

The middle school parent is as complex as the student. When the educator has made it their mission to reach parents, the students are the beneficiaries of a good relationship. There is a new set of parents to acclimate to the middle school environment every year. Each classroom teacher should be prepared to make his parents part of the education process. When we understand the parent and make them our ally, the students have full advantage of every adult.

Are you comfortable helping raise parents each year? Did you know that you would be an interpreter as well as a teacher? Did you know that you would have teammates in the education process?

PART THREE
THE EFFECTIVE SCHOOL

NINE

THE THRIVING SCHOOL

A middle school must have certain characteristics to function at a high level. The remainder of this book will focus on the essential qualities of an effective middle school. The qualities are by no means an exhaustive list, nor is this a how-to-manual. However, the characteristics describe any effective middle school.

After spending a majority of my adult life working in a middle school, I have determined that a middle school is either thriving or surviving. There really isn't another category. Those in the profession conceived the middle school concept about five decades ago. This was not a concept from an out-of-touch consultant or politicians trying to make a name for themselves. Many fly by-the-seat-of-our-pants programs are developed and handed down for hefty price tags every year. There is always a new program everyone needs to implement. Individuals who worked with students tried new initiatives and communicated with peers established the middle school concept. Initially, there were no attempts to get rich from the concept. I am sure they were thrilled to witness an environment where students were excited to come to school. I have been told it is the longest running movement in education and I have not been able to negate that claim. As I listened to several fathers of the movement speak at a national conference, I realized why it has been so successful. They did everything by trial and error. They were the pioneers. It wasn't an experiment in a vacuum; they were all vested in the venture of what is best for students. These leaders were feeding off one another to do what is best for their students and sharing their findings. They did what educators do best, stole one another's ideas and kept improving upon them.

The middle school movement has continued to grow over the last 50 years through trial and error, just as the early designers had experienced. Obviously, the movement is not a religion and this book makes no claims to perfection. However, through trial and error, there are some things that are very clear. Middle school students are different from high school and elementary students. It is the toughest age of life. It takes a special person to work with these students. There are proven strategies, structures, and beliefs that can make a school a nurturing and academically challenging environment where all students can find success.

Before the days of middle school were junior high schools, where students were treated as miniature high school students. They were created to bridge the gap between elementary and high school but never had a plan to address the needs of the middle child. Ultimately, it was obvious that 12-14-year-old students were much different and harder to reach than elementary children. For the safety and well-being of the elementary students, they needed to be separated. For the safety of these early adolescents and for the sanity of the high schools, they did not want to mix them with high school students. So that left us with a junior high school, kind of a holding pen, until they were old enough to go to high school. Students in elementary have a nurturing environment with the same teacher all day. Since they only have one teacher, they only follow one set of procedures and their personal items stay in their room for the entirety of the day. After sixth grade, they were transported straight to junior high. There was not a transitional period to junior high school. Junior high was a cold slap high school schedule with seven teachers, a locker, and different procedures for each class. You typically entered a junior high school as a seventh grade student. I was privileged to get to endure that brutal environment where students and teachers understood they were second-rate citizens for the duration of their junior high status. Locker rooms were a culture of their own, where the coach ignored inappropriate behaviors. There were also K-8 schools, which have seen success, with a continued nurturing environment. The positive of the K-8 is that students do not have to go through another transition. Some of these schools still exist and leaders have implemented middle school concepts as research develops. It is important that middle schools thrive by continuing to improve practices each year.

There are a plethora of best practices and identifying characteristics of a middle school. I will capture the most compelling characteristics of an effective middle school. Whether a school has all of the characteristics listed in the next few chapters does not make them a thriving school. *A thriving school is one that is moving in the right direction.* The name on a building means absolutely nothing when talking about a thriving middle school. Middle schools outnumber junior high schools 10-1, but that doesn't mean all middle schools are pursuing the best practices. Many so called "middle schools" couldn't tell you the first characteristic of a middle school. Some are just junior high schools that are configured 6-8th and have leaders who never taught a day in a middle school. Any group can change the name on the outside of a building with a school board vote. An effective middle school uses all of the stakeholders to create an environment using the best practices.

A middle school must have a vision. Not just a vision statement but a vision for what is best for students. Teachers should possess joy and passion because they get to make a difference in the lives of students. They are privileged to get to experience the journey with this group and make it a positive experience instead of a negative one. The school should bubble with an excitement from adults to students because they know they are on this journey together.

First and foremost, the question has to be asked, what is in the best interest of the student? Whether it be an individual academic question or a question of discipline, the school must ask, "What is best for the student?" When looking at the schedule, that question has to be asked. Every aspect of the school should revolve around what is best for the students. It is not about the comfort of the adults or the ease of the day. It is about students.

Schools tend to get influenced internally and externally by special interests. Schools are hounded by people trying to make their impact. Some people are trying to make money, some have a pet project they want to see get the most attention, and sometimes it is a selfish mentality of adults who want the world to be easier for them. If the leadership is strong, they will deflect anyone who is not seeking the student's best interest. When the question ceases to be what is best for students, you are going the wrong direction. It could be a matter of a company trying to let you know how to reach students using their approach, software, or materials. It could be a consultant who says your group should change the schedule in order to comply with their strategies. Sometimes a teacher wants their plan at a certain time because it suits them better. There has to be a mentality and culture established by leaders in the building that works for the best interest of their students.

In some districts, athletics or performing arts can become the focal point instead of the education of all students. An effective group of educators, when grouped together to collaborate in the best interest of students, is the most powerful tool in seeking effective ways to reach students academically and personally. Schools were not built for businesses to make a profit; they were built for students to gain knowledge. Whether it be food services, book distributors or professional consultants, they should only exist in your school if they are there to serve students. Performing arts and athletics are extremely important in the lives of our students, but their greatest interest is their field and should be considered as an equal peer in the stakeholder process. At no time should a special interest decide anything for a school building.

What is in the best interest of students can fall in to three basic categories: safety, academic, and personal. In order for students to thrive in middle school and continue to learn, they must feel safe. Students at any school should know that safety is the first priority. The first concern for administrators at any building should be student safety. Students in middle school should be monitored at all times. They should know that at no time are they alone. The procedures for students to enter the building, go to lunch, change classes, get permission to use the restroom, or exit to ride the bus home should demonstrate that student safety is the first priority. Obviously, they should be made to feel safe and loved. When a student feels safe, they will be able to perform at their personal best and be successful.

The initial purpose of a student attending a school is to gain knowledge. A thriving middle school challenges all students and encourages each child to push their limits of knowledge. Classrooms should be set up to meet the needs of every learning style. When determining anything academically for a student, the question should be, "What is in the best interest of the student?" Whether this be an individual student, or a group of students, we have to continue to ask the question. This will constantly put the focus on student learning. How will this group of students learn this concept best? What can I do to reach all students academically? When teachers are asking these questions, students will have the best classroom opportunities and the school will thrive.

Middle school students are a diverse group of children who come with their own set of quirks and needs. It is a sensitive time, where students have to be treated with kid gloves one minute and with a stern redirection the next minute. Each time, it has to be asked, "What does this student need? What is the best way to approach this child, correct this child or help this child?" Those who have never taught easily dismiss how a child feels about school, but it is critical that a child be comfortable. For example: a child stinks and their peers are complaining. This could seem like a simple fix, just tell them to take a shower. For anyone who thinks it is simple, and the response is the same to every child has little experience with middle school students. You could tell them to take a shower and even buy them a can of deodorant, but when you get the call from the angry parent later and a child refusing to come to school, you will reconsider your approach. The strategy that has to be used in every case is to get all of that child's educators in one place and ask, "What is the best way to approach this student?" For some, a teacher might be able to speak to them about the subject. For others, it is a counselor. For many, it is a call to their parents. Some students need to see an outside counselor who has the skills and the time to meet the needs of that child. No matter the approach, each child is different and many situations are sensitive.

In every case, we ask the question, "What is in the best interest of the student?" We start with safety and academics, but most of the time these questions become personal. In order for each child to thrive, we have to meet all of their needs sensitively. There isn't a quick solution or a systematic approach to meeting the individual needs of all students. We have to work with each student individually as needs arise.

In disciplinary measures, we ask, "What will cause this child to change their behavior?" Discipline can set the behavior tone for an entire building. Once upon a time, there was a theory to scare the students by making an example out of one. When a student did get in to trouble, we would punish that student. She might change her behavior because she doesn't like punishment. Although it sounds logical, so does the prison system, and that doesn't work in our society. We punish people and they continue to go back to prison. Most students do not need to experience fear in order to behave in the first place.

Discipline focuses on the child, punishment focuses on the behaviors. Discipline can range from counseling to in school suspension, but the goal at all times is for the child to be in the classroom learning with their peers. The question, "What will cause this child to change their behavior?" is the only question. This question and the ensuing answer will cause the adult asking to care about the well-being of the recipient of their decision. It's easy to throw a kid out with punishment; it is much more difficult to find yourself trying to figure out how a student operates and what he needs so he will behave in a way that does not interfere with other students. Thriving schools care about each child and remove distractions so learning can happen. Middle school students will make mistakes and have problems. How we deal with those mistakes and problems sets the tone for the building. Students should know and feel that we are working with them in their endeavors to grow up and become productive members of society.

A cornerstone of the middle school movement has been the interdisciplinary team. If a school is called a middle school, they must have interdisciplinary teams. Each group of 80-140 students will have the same core teachers. This can be set up a number of ways, but the most common setup is for the students' four core teachers to share the same students. These teams are able to integrate the curriculum. Teachers can flex the schedule to gain more instructional time when needed. Teachers can meet regularly to discuss student performance and behaviors. Teams will adopt common procedures so students will have the same procedures in every class. The interdisciplinary team will all share the same students, enabling them to connect and discuss the group as a whole. Students will also share classes with many of the same peers. This prevents students from getting lost. Teachers do not get lost either because they have a group of teachers to help support them. Teaming is a best practice for middle school. Middle Schools that thrive make teaming a priority.

A thriving middle school seeks smooth transitions for their students. Middle schools have to be prepared to transition their sixth graders to middle school and their eighth graders to high school. A school will thrive when students are prepared for the next step in their personal and academic career. In order for a school to prepare, they have to lay out all of the obstacles and fears students experience in order to make each transition smooth. It is all about perspective. If a sixth grade student is nervous about his locker because he hasn't tried it, he will not be in a good state of mind to learn in a classroom. Although a locker will be easy for these same students in a month, it is nerve-wracking for them the first few days of school. It will take practice for that student to feel comfortable getting in the locker and on time for the next class in five minutes. Students should be given multiple opportunities to practice before the first days of school. Teachers, counselors and administrators helping students every hour between classes the first few weeks of school is imperative. This is just one item that causes anxiety for our incoming students. Students are fearful of who they will sit with before school. Where will they put their band instrument? Will they be able to make it to the next class? Where are all of their classes? Will they have enough time to use the bathroom? Will they be able to go to the bathroom? What if they miss the bus? Who will get them? Transitions are a huge part of middle school and every item must be sensitively addressed.

Students also have anxiety about leaving middle school, especially if you have a good nurturing environment. It never fails; students will tell teachers they don't want to leave when they are in 8th grade. Thriving schools dissipate those fears by making them feel comfortable and excited to enter high school. Students visit their new school, both formally and informally, during their 8th grade year. They speak to the counselors, coaches, fine arts leaders and the principal. They enroll early and pick out their schedule. By the time a student leaves middle school, they should be plugged in to their next school and comfortable with the new adventures that await them. I think that is one of the beautiful things about being in the middle: you know it isn't the end. There is something just beyond the reaches of your door. As much as you might enjoy your students, you don't want them to stay with you. You know they are bound for something else, for somewhere else. They might cling to you because you are what they know and what they are comfortable with, but a thriving middle school also prepares them to walk confidently into the high school.

A thriving middle school continues to follow research and has a varied learning environment. Students should experience integrated instruction, collaborative learning groups, inquiry based learning and differentiated instruction. Students in a thriving middle school do not want to miss class because they will miss out on something fun and exciting. If there were ever a part of school considered the most important, the classroom would be the answer. The entire purpose of the existence of the school is because we want the students to learn. Seeking the best ways to reach the students and continuing to differentiate the curriculum is the foundation of a middle school.

Schools are built on their schedules, and middle schools are no exception. The middle school schedule can actually be a less complicated schedule, because teaming lends itself to simplicity. Middle schools that thrive are inclusive in their schedule design. Teacher representatives should be included in designing the schedule. The schedule of a middle school is built in the best interest of the students. Schedules must include built-in time for teachers to collaborate. If possible, entire grade levels should have built in times to collaborate in order for teachers to meet by discipline. Teachers are given a message by the way the leadership builds a schedule. If there is an expectation for teams and disciplines to meet in the best interest of the students, the principal will build in the time to make that possible.

A thriving middle school is full of employees who enjoy what they get to do every day. You know if a middle school is thriving or surviving when you talk to the teachers, the office staff, the cleaning staff, or the administration. When you walk into the office and are greeted by the face of the school, you get a good idea if the people working in the building are just there for their hours of duty, or if they are excited to welcome all of the visitors. You know when you call a child in sick if they care enough to inquire about their well-being. Teachers at a thriving school are excited to work with other equally competent teachers. Teachers can be fulfilled and experience enjoyment when they are a piece of the puzzle. There is an overall picture of success that they are able to contribute.

You know if it is a thriving middle school when the employees focus their conversations on the possible, not the impossible. I am not for sure anyone wants to listen to endless dialogue of why educators cannot be successful. There are also countless opportunities waiting to be discovered by diligent, creative educators pursuing their call to design lessons for all students to discover. People want to hear what the school is going to do for the children today. People need to hear about all of the wonderful lessons teachers are going to bring to the classroom. In a thriving school, educators proudly discuss the wonderful opportunities provided by their school. Teachers will boast of their successful lessons. They will even puff with pride over how they were able to construct their lesson within the means they were provided. Thriving educators see no boundaries; they see opportunities.

You will know a child is in a thriving school when the child comes home excited about school. The middle school child is extremely sensitive and very difficult to reach on a daily basis. For students to feel safe and to learn every day is a task that only a thriving school can accomplish. Students in thriving schools take pride in their schools and in their work. They are excited to wake up and come to school each day because they have a purpose. They enjoy the learning experience and realize they are in a unique place where they belong. They will brag about their school and take offense to anyone who criticizes their school.

Thriving middle schools make a difference in lives every day. Student success is the only option. The hallways and classrooms demonstrate student learning is taking place.

There is an excitement with all students and staff because they know each day is a great day to learn. Students grow from small children to adults and learn to become contributing members of their community. The effect that these schools have on their community is beyond measure.

It is not about the structure of the building; it is about the structure of the school. It is about the success of the students. Do the adults desire to be with this age group? A school is either thriving or surviving. They are either effective or they are not. It is also without question important that each middle school thrive because just to survive is unforgivable. The following chapters go in to detail the description of an effective middle school. All middle schools have the most precious commodity of our communities and should have a constant movement toward improving. A thriving school has a commitment to persevere for student best interests.

Is your school thriving or surviving? Where is the focus of the adults? Are the students the focal point? Do they ask the question, "what is in the best interest of this student?"

TEN

THE LEADER

An effective middle school has distinguished leadership that starts with the principal. All success or failures in the structure and initiatives of the school are the result of leadership. The principal shoulders all responsibility in the overall effectiveness of the school. Everything that occurs in the school will bear the name of the principal. Although principals are not directly responsible for reaching individual students, they are responsible for every person in the building and the direction of the staff as a whole. As to whether a school survives or thrives is up to the dedication of the leadership. I have witnessed principals just survive the day. I have heard of staff members wishing for a leader with a vision, energy, and passion. The principal is either an obstacle to innovation and progress or a conductor that energizes and boosts educators to success. Behind the scenes of every thriving middle school is an effective leader supporting the staff. Effective middle school principals have several characteristics in common.

The principal is the gatekeeper of the school. The gates cannot open unless it is necessary. Nobody has access to the teachers except through the principal. There is no possible way teachers could perform their duties if every person who walked through the door received the attention they demanded. There must be no outside influences get to the students except through the principal. Many well-intentioned people wish to speak to the students about the dangers of drinking or drugs or bullying. Although some causes are deemed worthy to be granted time with students, more often they are turned away in favor of instructional time. Unfazed by the law or reality, some parents wish to confront students and are in amazement that is not an option for them. I once had a parent who came to eat lunch with their child, which is not only allowed but encouraged. While eating, I noticed he was staring at another child. I pulled the parent aside and asked why he kept staring at a different child. He told me stories about a conflict with this child and his own. He was extremely surprised that I asked him to leave and never come past the office again. He had no idea it was not okay to stare down a student in the cafeteria. The principal is the protector of the school. They are the guards who make sure no person gets through the school doors who have no legitimate business accessing students. The principal is the gatekeeper of all distractors and threats.

A middle school leader should have middle school experience. In some districts, the school superintendent puts someone in charge of a middle school with no understanding of this age group or the abilities to reach them. The principal of a middle school should have middle school teaching experience. If he has classroom experience, he will understand the students, teachers, and parents of the middle school child. He will have intimate knowledge of the middle school concept, schedule, and productive programs. If a principal did not have teaching experience in middle school, it would be difficult for him to evaluate teachers and render him an ineffective instructional leader. In order for a middle school to thrive, there must be an effective leader.

Just like any educator, the principal or leader of the middle school must be called to this age group. She must be able to relate to middle school students. She should have a desire to be a middle school principal. She has to know her position fills a great need. The principal must be dedicated to the cause of reaching all students, academically and socially. An effective principal has a level of dedication and ownership similar to clergy. She knows her job never ends and she will take it home at night. It is part of life. The position of principal should be a destination they aspire to fill and make a difference. It should not be a rung on the ladder while they wait for a central office position. A principal has to inspire her constituents. It isn't enough to tell people what you believe to be important, you have to show them what is important.

The principal controls the environment. The environment of the school is a direct reflection of leadership. The leader must be a great communicator. The principal must be able to get the attention of students, teachers and parents. In order to be promoted to a principal, he should be a master at communicating with students. It takes a special person to be able to communicate with an entire school and keep their attention. Teachers seem like an easy group to communicate with, but they can be a challenging audience because they get busy, distracted with lesson plans that truly are important, and they are generally just like their students with short attention spans. A leader is tasked with holding a group of teachers accountable while staying respectful. It is easier to captivate the attention of 700 students at one time than 45 teachers, however, a principal must communicate clearly to his staff if he has any expectation to lead the school. The parents are the most difficult because, unlike students and teachers, it is impossible to reach all of them. They are not forced to be at school. A leader must be able to convey information to all groups and will become accustomed to whatever means possible to communicate with parents.

A highly effective middle school principal builds leadership capacity with all of his constituents. In order to build capacity, the constituents have to know every decision focuses around the best interest of students. This does not happen in a staff meeting, through emails, or a blog. Demonstrating to constituents that your focus is in the best interest of students happens each day with every decision. Teachers, secretaries, parents and students are watching, listening and doing basic reconnaissance missions daily determining the motives of the principal's every move. If a leader is self-serving, playing favorites, too busy, ignorant to the age group, or pushing an agenda, she will not be able to build capacity.

When a leader has a meeting with a group of parents, they should come away knowing the leader cares about students. Parents should know and trust the principal's judgment and decisions. Parents want their children to have the best middle school experience. Most of them are just trying to figure out their own child. They need to see and hear that the leader has put their best foot forward in all aspects. They need assurance their babies will be taken care of by professionals. An effective leader will educate parents on the best practices for middle school. Parents also want their children to have opportunities for wholesome activities. Effective principals work with parents to plan appropriate activities for students.

Although students will follow the direction of the principal because the position dictates their cooperation, *effective principals build a trust with students.* Great leaders explain their decisions to their students and make sure they know their best interests are always the determining factor. Students will get angry when they can't go outside for lunch. When the leader explains that the wind chill factor is the cause, the students respect the decision. When the principal tells the students they must be quiet while entering the building because there are other students in class and the noise will cause a distraction, the students will self-police and support the administrator. If you just tell students to be quiet with no explanation, they will oblige until you turn your back. Middle school students can process information and make conclusions like young adults. When possible, it is great to involve students in the decision making process. In order to build leadership capacity, a principal must relate to the students. It is important a leader knows his students. It is great for a principal to get on the playground and join the students. Playing a game of foursquare, basketball or tetherball with students changes the way students perceive their leader. Catching a pass thrown by your principal or sitting next to him on the swing set for a minute can redefine a student's opinion. School leaders should be in the hallway talking with students daily. Every opportunity a leader can create to stay in touch with students is monumental in their quest to serve those students. Students in an effective middle school know their principal and feel comfortable sharing ideas and concerns.

Teachers are the most difficult group to build leadership capacity because they cannot be snowballed. You cannot fake student best interest. You must be well-versed in strategies to reach middle school teachers. They are not impressed with leaders who just toe the company line and repeat the expectations of the central office. Teachers need to be treated as experts and professionals by principals. They expect to have a stake in any decision made on behalf of students. The centerpiece of every conversation should be student interest. It takes time before teachers will collectively trust a building administrator. In order to enact change, bring in a new program, or just change a simple hallway procedure that involves staff, you must build trust amongst your teachers. They will be the catalyst to successful change in school.

Effective school administrators acknowledge the importance of the classroom. Every job outside of the classroom is meant to support what happens in the classroom. That understanding must be conveyed consistently in a building. A successful middle school that is effectively reaching students academically and personally has an instructional leader in the front office. There have been entire books written on instructional leadership. The principal must put instruction first when making decisions. The focus of everything in a building should support the classroom. The principal has to lead that concept in their building. The schedule is developed with maximization of classroom instruction. No office personnel, including the administrators, counselors, cafeteria, library or janitors take precedence over the classroom needs. Even the superintendent, board members, and directors exist to support the classroom. The teachers are the front line to the students. Every other position supports their position. This does not take away from any other person, but their positions are supportive of the classroom, including the building leader. They know this when they are hired. When that concept is accepted throughout the building, it becomes much easier to bring focus to student learning. An instructional leader sets the tone for the school to put instruction first. An instructional leader is not a stranger to the classroom. They visit classrooms consistently and know the strengths of each teacher. The leader will also know the classroom needs.

The most important task of any principal is to hire the most qualified instructors. These individuals will be spending seven and a half hours every school day with children. Students will spend more time with their teachers than with their parents during the week.

Teachers affect students greatly. Teachers play a significant role in the lives of their students and can affect them both academically and personally. Teachers should be vetted during the interview process. A school leader needs to have the gift of discernment. They have to know whether a teacher will work well with their students. It isn't enough to just trust one interview impression. References have to be called and social media outlets have to be explored in order to find out if the candidate has the skills to work with children. Every possible avenue to research their character needs to be explored. They can have an effect for a lifetime and it needs to be positive.

A teacher candidate must be able to handle a classroom of middle school students and the principal has to determine their capabilities. During the interview process, the building leader must lay out all expectations for the potential candidate to buy in and commit. If there is an expectation for the position to do extra duties, the interview is the time to gain that buy-in from the candidate. Beyond character and classroom control, the teacher candidate needs the knowledge and skills to differentiate the instruction to a diverse group of students. The candidate must also be able to communicate with adults, both parents and colleagues. They will be working on a teaching team and expected to communicate daily with other teachers on their team. There are teachers who can do a good job in the classroom but lack in their ability to communicate with their peers. They will not survive in an effective middle school where collaboration is highly valued. I witnessed a teacher who could not carry on a conversation with another adult in the building without conflict, but she did a good job in the classroom. Her team suffered and there was constant tension. I heard she is doing well in another district where she doesn't have to communicate with others. In an effective middle school, you must work well with every group. If only I had caught her problem with adult interactions during the interview process, I would have saved a year of misery for that teaching team.

The principal should treat the hiring process like a college recruiter after an athlete. They should be trying to fill their position by calling universities or asking other teachers in the building if they are aware of possible candidates. Middle school principals must seek the best candidates. They cannot just post the position and expect the most qualified candidates to come running to their door. When a teacher is not meeting expectations, the principal must be forthright and let the teacher find another career path. It is an injustice to students to allow a teacher who is subpar to stay in their position. If a teacher is lacking classroom control, teaching abilities, or character, it is the responsibility of the principal to communicate this to the teacher and open their position for a better candidate. If the teacher is tenured, they need a plan of improvement until the school board can terminate. The same would be said for a janitor, teacher's aide, or a secretary. If they are not kind-hearted and supportive of the classroom, they should be given a direct opportunity to find another career path. All students deserve the best and middle school students need the best.

A great leader appreciates those who make them look good. When there are effective instructors, hardworking janitorial staff members, and kind office staff, the job of the principal becomes simpler and more effective. The leader should let his staff know they're appreciated. Most of the time, an educator is fairly amused by the smallest token of appreciation. Educators are not accustomed to bonuses, profit sharing, and company vacations. A pat on the back and a free lunch are like finding gold in most schools. A leader has to be in tune with her staff. Many parent groups and businesses are just a phone call away from helping. Teachers are thrilled with a thank you and a meal orchestrated by their leader. An effective leader understands the staff desire to feel a level of appreciation and meets those needs. I remember teaching at a school and getting a free lunch. It made my day. Providing a lunch, a cup with the school name or a t-shirt is more about priority than money. Teachers love appreciation from their leader but value kind words and gestures from students and families affected by their dedication and sacrifice. A caring principal will seek out opportunities for students and parents to extend their recognition to their teachers. It can be as simple as a letter from a student to the teacher. A leader can even suggest that the parents write a teacher a thank you note during Teacher Appreciation Week. Teachers don't work because they think they will get monetary gifts; it is because they know they have a positive effect on the life of a child. It is a beautiful thing when the student has the opportunity to express their appreciation to the teacher. The school leader should be instrumental in organizing those opportunities on a consistent basis.

An effective leader trusts the educators that work in their building. There isn't another profession that is overloaded with highly educated individuals who are working for less than they could make in another profession. They feel called to their position and should be treated with a level of trust. In Finland, the world's leader in test scores, the teachers are trusted to perform their duties without stringent evaluations. Their evaluations are informal. They believe if there is a problem, the students and parents will let them know. Coming from seventeen years of middle school experience, parents and students will let you know if there is a problem in a classroom long before a formal evaluation will expose such an issue. Although a leader must follow the law with evaluations, teachers should feel trusted in their classrooms. Effective teachers are well aware of their deficiencies and can let you know quickly any area they feel a need to improve. An effective leader highlights a teacher's strengths through consistent encouragement and support. They work through any weaknesses and deficiencies through training and support. Teachers desire success. Their success directly affects the lives of students every day. In order to keep the best teachers in a building, teachers must feel trusted and respected.

The day it was announced I would be promoted to principal in my building, a local education icon and community leader came by to congratulate me. He had been in education over fifty years and retired from two states. He even came out of retirement to serve a short stint as my interim boss. He looked me in the eye and said, "Joey, I know a lot of people in this town. People talk to me all of the time. The one thing that they all say about you is that you have common sense. That man has common sense." I wasn't sure how to take his comments. It seemed to be a compliment, but most people want to hear intelligent, leadership, and innovative in the description. I have come to appreciate his comments more every day. You hear people talk about school leadership all of the time. They consistently marvel about the way a child was treated. The systematic approach to their child's discipline is ridiculous. The wasteful ways in which the school is spending the taxpayer's money. The ridiculous redundancy in the classes a child has to take. It all boils down to common sense. Common sense means that you think like the common person. *A leader has to put himself in the shoes of the person he is serving*. If it is a child, he puts himself in those small shoes. If it is a parent, he thinks how she would feel and what makes sense for her. If it is the public image in general, a principal must understand the perception of each decision. If the leader thinks in the best interest of the child, everyone will most often agree.

The leader of the school must lead by example. If

you have an expectation of teachers in a building, the principal should be able to lead the way. If the principal expects adults to differentiate the instruction, they should be able to show them by taking their class for an hour. A principal should have been a stellar teacher before taking an administrative position in the first place. If the leader wants the staff to be trained in a program, they should join them in the training. If there is an initiative to involve students in clubs, the leader should lead the way in starting a club. The principal should have strong beliefs as an educator. She should be able to back up those beliefs with the skills and commitment to see it be successful.

Each school has initiatives they have adopted to be successful. In order for an initiative to be successful, it must be born of a collaborative approach from stakeholders. When a group makes a decision to move forward and adopt an approach to reach students, the school leader must lead the way in implementing the initiative. They must also have the stamina to stick with the initiative and see it to success. I have witnessed a school take on three initiatives and continue to perfect them over 20 years. They are highly successful because they have great leadership. They also have managed to avoid major pressure to implement the latest greatest program. When a program is implemented from the top down to solve a problem that a distant leader believes will be the answer, another expensive program in a short time will replace it. Teachers get weary of new training and new programs that will save the day. There has to be a strong leader who keeps the focus on students, not programs. When an initiative is successful, teachers have buy in to the implementation, and the school leader must have the strength to support the movement.

A principal of an effective school will continuously give credit to those who work so hard with the students. Any school leader must acknowledge he rarely does anything worthy of credit, except put the right people in position to be successful and support them. An effective leader will redirect any accolades to the dedicated professionals who answer the call and make a difference in the lives of students each day. A great leader will promote the positive aspects of the school, highlighting the people responsible for each success. There are leaders in pursuit of undue credit. They are usually the micromanagers that continue to stifle the creativity and imaginations of all those under them. They want to hang around and pat each other on the back while attributing their hard work was the factor for any successes achieved by those who work for them.

An effective school leader is direct, approachable, passionate and resourceful. A successful leader of a middle school is direct about the mission, procedures, and initiatives of the school. They handle each situation with authority and decisiveness. There is not an adult or student who will stand in the way of safety or compromise the mission of the school. The principal is the face of the school and will deliberately confront any situation that threatens the effectiveness of the building.

The leader is approachable to all parties. Parents feel comfortable with the leader of the building and will bring attention to any concerns they have personally or collectively. Teachers know they can bring student concerns to the attention of the principal and have faith they can give effective feedback from personal experience. They can also approach a principal about procedures, classroom control, and instruction, with confidence the leader will help them with a broad repertoire of strategies. Most importantly, students can approach the principal with ideas or concerns to help the school become a better functioning environment.

Great leaders are passionate. The passion of an effective middle school principal will be to provide the best environment for students and teachers to thrive.

Every personality is different, but every effective school leader is passionate about the success of all students in a safe environment. A passionate leader will find the resources to be successful. Whether it be grant writing or finding the right connection of individuals, an effective leader is resourceful for her school.

One of the greatest callings in life is to lead a middle school. A middle school is an important place to affect students; it is criminal for someone to work in the school if he is not highly effective. A leader who belongs will take honor in filling the position. Students will remember middle school for the rest of their lives. It is the most awkward and strangest time of anyone's childhood experience and they all deserve a leader who belongs in the middle. A leader who will interact with them and make it a great experience. An individual who will bring an excitement and charisma to the position every day because they enjoy the students they have the opportunity to affect. An instructional leader who cares that every day is filled with exciting new opportunities to learn and enjoy the middle school experience. Every middle school deserves a leader who belongs in the middle.

Does the leader of your school put student interest first? Is the principal of your school an instructional leader? Are they the gatekeeper? Can the leader hire effective teachers? Are they called to the middle?

ELEVEN

THE EFFECTIVE ENVIRONMENT

Every person who has entered a school knows there is a feeling you get when you open the door. You can define it to a smell or the décor before you even see a face. The feelings continue as you have contact with more people. You either get a positive or negative vibe and it magnifies with the length of the visit. Everyone has lingering emotions of how s/he felt as a student in school, especially middle school. However, all of those feelings subside when you enter an effective middle school. There is an expectation that every school should be open and welcoming, caring and friendly. Obviously, that is not always the case, but one thing is for sure, you know it when you walk through the door.

Dr. Jim Faye tells us that a school is run on either principles or systems. He explains in his book, *Love and Logic for Educators*, that you can tell when you enter a school whether they take a systematic approach to leading their school or a principled approach. He goes on to mention systems are great for pilots of airplanes, but we need a school to be directed by principles. It took me months to digest that particular chapter of his book because I began to reflect and question my own methodology in every approach that I take in our middle school. After much reflection, I determined that every possible approach that is not bound by systematic law must be principled. When there is a principled approach to the school, the school environment is much more effective. If you have an effective school environment, it is because there is a principled approach. A principled approach to school means that we work directly with people and their individual situation. We answer our phones and listen, instead of letting a computer direct people. We do not believe there is a system that can effectively run a school. If you are in a tornado drill, a systematic approach to safety is completely understandable and expected. If you are dealing with discipline, you had better talk to each child individually to help change their behavior because systems have proven completely ineffective. Take zero tolerance policies for example. It sounded like a great idea to have a blanket district discipline policy for weapons so every student would be safe and treated fairly. There is a difference between a sixth grader having a steak knife packed in her lunch (with leftover steak) and a senior bringing a hunting knife in his backpack with ill intentions. It doesn't make any sense for both to receive the same discipline. Under a systematic approach to discipline both students get arrested and suspended for the remainder of the year. Under the principled approach to discipline the parent of the sixth grader gets a harsh phone call and the senior gets suspended and goes to jail.

An effective school has a friendly environment in the office, the hallways, and the classroom. It is immediately apparent whether a school cares about the constituents they serve. An effective thriving school has a friendly environment that cares about public interest. When a parent calls to inquire about a grade, a tardy, a discipline or a course change, they should be greeted by a friendly voice directing them to someone who can answer their questions. When someone enters a school, a knowledgeable individual who is friendly and can direct them the right way with a smile should greet them. There is a complete difference in the way that a person will feel about the school by the way they are treated in the office. The importance of a friendly face to greet visitors as they enter a building cannot be underscored. I have entered schools that did not have anyone available to greet the public. I have walked hallways with no acknowledgement that I had entered the premises. Office staff have treated me sarcastically. I have also been instrumental in the removal of an individual who treated people rudely and disrespectfully. The office can be a completely different place with the simple removal of one individual. A teacher who can't handle students has less of an impact on public perception than office personnel who are rude to the patrons. The mass majority of visitors to enter a school never make it past the office. I have seen amazing office personnel who serve up a smile and respect with every person regardless of class. I have seen unshakeable strength despite the lack of tact by the public. The office staff that puts the student interest first does not let adults affect them. The impact made by the individuals who work in the office of a school is immeasurable. An effective school will be welcoming and friendly in every room of the building, including the office.

One of the most important tasks of school personnel is to establish an effective culture. Effective middle schools make character education a staple of their curriculum. It could be through a mentoring program; it could be through a program such as Great Expectations, Tribes, or one of the many other character education models. Some schools make up their own curriculum. Regardless of the source, there needs to be curriculum where all adults can use the same vocabulary with students. Students must learn how to treat other students and adults. When they come to school, there has to be a culture of kindness and respect towards all other individuals. An adult in the building will correct anything outside of the accepted behavior. The common sarcasm and put-downs heard in the hallways of some schools and the local mall will not be tolerated in an effective middle school. This has to be reinforced by the leader. All students treat others with mutual respect.

Character education must include mutual respect, honesty, kindness and caring. Although these are not an exhaustive list of character traits, it is a huge undertaking for any institution. Mutual respect can be responsible for the majority of behavior issues in somebody's social life. If every student treated another with mutual respect, we wouldn't have a disciplinary issue in schools. When we teach students to be honest, it will help them not only make a better environment for the school, but improve their credibility at home and with future employers. When students are kind and caring toward one another, they develop personal skills to put other people before themselves. These are not easy traits to teach and it takes perseverance on the part of the educator. It is more about expectations for the students. Teachers are consistently using daily examples to amplify these character traits. Most importantly, all adults in the building are modeling the traits they desire the students to possess.

When an effective school culture has been established, students feel safe and it is apparent throughout the entire school. In order for there to be any learning achieved in a school building, students must feel safe. Personal safety is many times classified with just physical safety. While physical safety is important, peer mistreatment inhibits student performance on a daily basis if there is not an established culture of respect. In an effective school, students feel comfortable presenting and performing in front of others because a culture of mutual respect has been established.

When students learn character through a common language and established culture, bullying is eliminated from their environment. Bullying cannot flourish in an effective environment. An effective school is a safe school. This is the age when students will push the boundaries. They are trying to figure out how they are supposed to act in situations. An effective school lets the students know when they cross the line. The seeds of bullying will not find fertile ground in an effective environment. There is no tolerance for intimidation. The general student population appreciates the feeling of safety and will tell an adult when someone is not being treated appropriately. When you walk down the hallways of an effective middle school, students are walking and talking at appropriate levels because there are procedures in place that allow students to understand their boundaries. Students want their hallways to be safe. They understand it is expected that they treat others respectfully. There are adults watching at every turn to make sure the students are staying within their boundaries.

Safe school environments are monitored. Students know when adults are observing their behavior, and it is imperative there are always adults monitoring middle school students. Procedures are the boundaries in which students may live. When appropriate procedures have been established in the hallways, cafeteria, and playground, there will be a safe environment for all students.

When expectations of character and procedures have been established, the school becomes a safe haven for all. Students are friendly, adults are friendly, and the world of middle school becomes a utopia. This is how all middle schools should operate. This is where teachers want to work. This is where students want to attend school.

An effective middle school has an inclusive environment. Students are willing to help a new student become acclimated. Students are inclusive and helpful because they are proud of their environment. It is much easier to show the new student to their locker, the lunch line, and the classrooms because you don't have to apologize for the mistreatment they will endure in the future.

An effective middle school has a culture of learning. During a professional development meeting a consultant said, "We want students to learn." A veteran teacher responded by saying, "Don't worry, students are always learning." He was right. They are always learning, but are they absorbing what we want them to learn? Are they focusing out the window or on something that has piqued their interest in the classroom? Are they digesting or are just regurgitating information?

Are they processing information? The purpose of schools is student learning and that concept is not lost in an effective middle school environment. If students are actively engaged in learning, the culture of the school will immediately improve. If teachers have been properly trained and understand student engagement, their task of student learning becomes much simpler. Every classroom and teacher are different, and they should all be meeting learning styles. Every aspect of a school should be centered on student learning. The budget expenditures should justify student learning. The schedule should revolve around student learning. The building layout should be in the best interest of student learning.

Middle schools have frequent visitors, whether they be consultants, parents or visitor shadows, and the students do experience adults in the building on a regular basis. Madison Middle School has invited key public figures for the last decade to shadow students as part of Middle Level Education Month, a nationwide initiative. It has been amazing to hear the responses from the wide range of individuals who have shadowed. Most have not been in a middle school since they were fourteen and they always have a nervous tension before starting their day. I have never heard a negative response from a shadow about the culture of the students. They are always amazed and wish they had experienced middle school in this culture. Effective schools invite adults to the classroom. They want visitors to join the learning experience. Students eagerly greet visitors and assist them with the assignment or project they are working to complete. Students are welcoming and polite. They are the ambassadors of the school.

An effective environment has an energy. Middle schools are exciting atmospheres with students expending their energy in every direction. When a school is a safe and positive place to learn, students are excited to be there. It is no secret that many homes are not positive or exciting. Some are downright abusive. Many students come to school and experience a different culture than they are accustomed. They are respected and loved. They want to be there because it makes them feel good. They know they will be treated fairly and they feel safe. Students enjoy being at school and the learning process becomes part of the joy of their life. Some students don't want to leave at the end of the day.

The environment defines the school. Adults control the environment of the school, both cultural and physical. The school leader and teachers are completely responsible for the cultural environment. That is a heavy load for a group of adults to bear, but it is the truth. The cultural environment affects students. It will affect the learning environment and the public's perception of the school.

The environment of a school is founded upon the culture that has been established by leadership. Effective atmospheres have a culture of learning, mutual respect, kindness, helpfulness, calmness, and safety. The culture of the school can be detected the moment you enter the building. Everyone is aware you get a perception when you open the door to a school. From the moment you enter the door, you are either comfortable or defensive. You feel either students are the priority or you want to choke some sense in to someone. The school environment is structured in the best interest of the students or the staff. An effective school has a staff that structures the school in the best interest of the students.

When student learning is the focus, there is a calmness in the environment. Although it is no secret that middle school students can definitely be excitable when on their best behavior, they are calming in their focus. Effective educators harness the excitement and energy toward learning. The hallways are calmer in a school where the classroom environment is active. Students achieve in the classroom and their energy is positively directed. When there is a focus on learning, the discipline dissipates. It is wonderful when few students are sent to the office because students are too busy in the classroom.

Just like the cultural environment, the physical environment is also controlled by adults. The physical environment of the hallways and classrooms is in complete control of the local school employees. The saying "cleanliness is next to godliness" is a little over used but almost applicable in this scenario. There is absolutely no excuse for a school to be dirty. All learning environments should be clean. The physical environment is in complete control of the leader and teachers. The walls should make everyone feel comfortable. From the color of the walls to the items displayed on the walls, they should be welcoming, teaching and celebrating. There are many studies that show colors make a difference in student moods. When I was an assistant principal, I walked in to a room that was painted fluorescent yellow. I went straight to the principal and asked if she had given permission to paint the room. I told her of the horrible color and my inability to concentrate just looking at the room. I did tell her that there are many studies showing that calming colors help students concentrate. The color of a room and the displays on the wall are extremely important. The colors should be calming and the walls should display meaningful content and student personal best work. The principal and teachers should be consistently monitoring what the walls are telling our students.

The physical condition of the building is the responsibility of the superintendent. There are some buildings that are beautiful. There are some that are in dire need of repairs. I have worked in both. Although aggravating, because it most definitely reflects in the public perception of the school, it is not the local school employee's responsibility. Some buildings are completely judged by the outside appearance. The focus of the principal and teachers must be on the cultural environment of the school. I once worked in a building that local realtors claimed was under construction because the roof was coming off and it looked horrible. People new to town would ask why it looked so horrible. Some people thought it was already abandoned on days that school was not in session. Fortunately, if the new arrivals would ever make it into the school, they would appreciate the culture established in the building. Students quickly forget what a building looks like, whether good or bad, and begin to focus on what a building feels like.

It is a work of art to see a middle school come together to form a positive safe learning environment where all students can enjoy the middle school experience. It is not an easy feat, but nothing short of an effective environment is fair to our constituents. Students only get this opportunity once and we owe it to each child to create the best environment possible for them to experience the middle years.

What kind of environment does your school have? Do others comment positively or negatively about your school environment? Are the office personnel friendly?

TWELVE

CONNECTIONS

There is perhaps no greater cause in a school than to connect to a child. Although most teachers would give a politically correct answer if asked the question why they chose a career in education, the honest answer would be because they want to positively affect students. They want connection. Although teachers are consistently being driven for test results, actual progress measured by standardized testing will take a drop if students do not have a connection. Real progress is seeking to connect with every student.

Connections are fairly simple in elementary schools by nature of the setup, with one teacher for every twenty-five students. Classrooms are self-contained, so the students usually don't have more than one teacher, except for electives. Teachers develop a relationship with their students and they are responsible for their class. The teacher takes on the role of parent at school for their students. If there is a problem with a student, it is easily identifiable.

After elementary, students begin to change. When they start puberty, the personality and physical stature of the child accelerates and twists. Parents who thought they knew their children begin to disconnect. Even the sweetest of children get their parents' attention during the middle years.

In our school district, along with about every district in America, we were asked to do a dropout prevention study and put measures in place that would help our students make choices to stay in school. Until No Child Left Behind, most dropouts were basically ignored on the basis that the students had made their choices. The dropout students were most likely problem students anyway. Once money and school report cards were tied to the results of the dropouts, districts pulled out all of the stops to keep students in schools. Our high school principals found it very effective to track the students down once they quit attending. The leaders would knock on their door and convince them to come back. If that didn't work, every relative was contacted until they were annoyed back to the building. Leaders also found students would likely attend if given an option to take classes online or take the GED. We were asked what we would do as a middle school to help with the dropouts.

As a committee, we spent many months discussing what we should do to help our students. It is rare for a student to even attempt to drop out in middle school, so that was an easy task. But what about these same students when they left us? We knew many were at risk and we wanted to help keep them in school for the duration of high school. We learned a simple fact: students who are connected to school are more likely to graduate. Whether it be because they love school, sports, music or a club, if they have something that connects them to school, they will be more likely to walk across the stage in a few short years. We also learned that studies have shown that many students will make a choice to drop out of school by the fourth grade, even though they cannot do so for more than five years. It is engrained in their mind that they will not graduate.

Students connect to school in a multitude of ways. The most important part of the connection is not the activity, but the person leading the activity. Students connect to adults through their interests. This brings to light the importance of character in every adult in the building. When thinking about student connections, the first thing that comes to mind for most people is sports. Sports have done a phenomenal job connecting students to school for over a century. They subsequently teach students how to compete, handle success and failure, participate on a team, and learn to obey authority. Sports have been the saving grace for so many students, particularly the underprivileged class. Sports are becoming much less about participation and more about the intensity of winning. Because of this level of competition, fewer students are being included to participate for the schools. The high school team is expected to be chosen in middle school. The pressure is on the coaches to win and they need to know which students to develop. Consequently, there are a large group of subpar athletes who get left out of the shuffle before they even enter high school.

Students who are part of the fine arts department are also less likely to drop out of school because they have made a connection through their chosen group. Students who join the band or orchestra are fortunate to get to learn how to play an instrument. That is possibly one of the greatest benefits of public education. Students who learn to play an instrument are able to make connections in their brain that allow them to learn more information. Students who are in band are stereotypically smart. By high school, they adopt their own chosen culture, but it is not an overstatement to say many students in band would have dropped out of school because of boredom. Band captures many students who are right-brained-artsy and not particularly stressed out to get their homework turned in unless there is a consequence beyond a bad letter on their report card. Band has saved a multitude of students in the last century and kept those students connected until they could reach college where the majority can flourish. Some students fortunate enough to have the opportunity have chosen to join orchestra. In our school system, it is as popular as band and reaches another group of students who are not particularly connected to anything else. These are students who may not want to march at five o'clock every morning and would prefer to play a stringed instrument. They are also able to make those brain connections that allow them to retain more information. All school systems should encourage every student to play an instrument. If anyone is in touch with brain research, the benefits of playing an instrument cannot be ignored.

Although athletics and fine arts have truly blessed youth for generations, there is over half of the student population in need of something different. Our connections committee brainstormed and researched what other opportunities we could offer our students that would connect them with middle school. What do students need? What do they enjoy? What would make them feel connected? What does connect a student? After much research and brainstorming, we categorized student connectedness outside of the regular offerings of athletics and arts in to three categories. These three categories can also intertwine, depending on the group. *Students can connect to school through clubs, community service, and mentoring.* All middle schools should offer the opportunity for students to connect and we have set out to make sure they get these opportunities.

Although a certain group of clubs have been staples for years in middle school, they have only been able to reach a small percentage of students. Student groups such as student council, academic club, chess club, drama and yearbook are a few that have existed in middle school for a long time. As a model, those clubs have shown a dedication and connection from students. Some clubs require passing grades in order to participate, but most have traditionally allowed students to attend. The outlet for students to demonstrate leadership and creativity while building relationships with an adult has been very beneficial to the handful blessed with the opportunity to join. Students have attributed these opportunities to their success reached later in life.

Upon the realization the level of impact clubs could

have on students, our group set out to develop as many opportunities as possible for students to participate at our school. It started with each member starting a club and selling the concept to the staff. With zero funds available, we had to utilize all resources within our grasp. We had a builder's club using the old shop equipment from the days of old. We had crafting, running, business, archery and robotics clubs. When we were finished with the inaugural year, we had started twelve new clubs and involved over 100 students. It was a success, and we knew we were on to something. Although it is loosely organized and funding is very limited from our parent support group, clubs have grown over the years. Just like any good initiative, it takes time to make it part of your culture. When we interview teachers, we tell them about our clubs and goals to reach all students. We ask them if they will consider starting a club if they are hired. I initially feared that potential candidates would run from the expectation of the level of dedication involved in starting a club. To the contrary, teachers have embraced the opportunity to contribute.

I have learned teachers appreciate being part of a group effort to reach students. This is not under the guise that test scores will increase or that we will ever mandate that a teacher will participate. The club initiative is designed for teachers to have the opportunity to enjoy an activity with students and connect to them. The opportunity to pick something they enjoy doing and invite students to join once a week has proven extremely rewarding. When the majority of the staff is also contributing, it becomes part of the culture of the building. The charge from teachers to teachers has been to start a club. Whether it be once a week or once a month. It could be in the morning, lunchtime or after school. Get involved and invite students.

After the first year, students began to ask about clubs before the first day of school. New sixth graders are excited to get involved and join. We offer everything from culinary to bowling. We have had geocaching, Harry Potter lunch bunch and Holiday crafting. We have completed the sixth year of this initiative and have had over thirty club opportunities for students each of the past five years. The creativity coming from the minds of the majority of teachers is more than we could have ever dreamt up on our own. Some clubs play, some clubs work, some clubs serve and some clubs create. There are clubs that cook for themselves and some that cook to give to others. Teachers decide what they would like to offer and the students sign up. We finally started collecting some data. More than 60% of the student body participates in a club. We did not make that huge connection six years ago. Students are demanding when they approach us about club opportunities. They have a need to connect and we have met the needs of the students. They believe it is their absolute right and we have not corrected them because we are happy they are connected through this endeavor.

I was recently at a conference where a colleague presented his new initiative for clubs. His clubs are built in to the school day once a week. They are participating in maker's clubs, where students create things. They have used available technology and concentrate on inventing things. Teachers in his school have also chosen what they would like to do. Just like the teachers in Bartlesville, there is buy in because they are doing something to reach students. They have 100% participation from their student body because it is during the school day. They have very few discipline problems because the kids are involved in activities they enjoy. At a former school where I taught, they have a program called extended day, where students who ride the bus stay for an extra 45 minutes each day. Para teachers and some teachers are asked to teach a course in an area of interest. Students are not given grades and it is very similar to clubs.

Effective middle schools create opportunities for students to develop interests. Leaders of the school pave the way for those opportunities to come to fruition. In my school, the principal and assistant principal have a weekly club. If the school leaders are not out in front modeling the initiative, the majority of the staff will not understand the importance. Clubs have blown up in to something we could never have imagined because the students were hungry for the opportunity.

The second area that our committee chose to concentrate is community service or volunteer service. We define volunteer service as performing a service for an organization or individuals who are not family that does not result in compensation. Volunteerism connects students to the school. I have had many projects throughout my years in school administration that I have depended on the help of students to complete. I was given permission to pursue building an outdoor learning environment at our middle school. After careful planning, we began raising the funds, mostly for supplies because we felt we could build most of it ourselves. Before I realized it, I was in way over my head and needed help. I was preparing for one of the grants we had received and met a parent on the weekend at the school. We needed to dig a hole in the ground for a water feature. We had to have it done that weekend for grant requirements. It was 37 degrees with high wind. The hole was supposed to be four foot squared by two foot deep. The ground was solid rock and it was cold. A young man by the name of Grant stopped by out of nowhere. This seventh grader was just wandering on his bike through the school grounds bored on a Saturday morning. He happened upon us digging and getting weary. Grant asked us if we wanted any help. Except for one physical altercation where he was disciplined, I had no relationship or communication with this student. We told him that he was welcome to stay and help. He stayed with us the entire time taking turns with the pry bar and shovel. It took us 6 hours to complete that hole where the water feature is now located.

For the next year I had students at the school working on the OLE every day, evening, and weekend. I had student aides who helped build during one hour of the day. Teachers led crews of students on specific projects. Grant met me every day after school his 8th grade year. Most of it was serious grunt work moving wheelbarrows full of dirt, lifting cinder blocks, digging rocks, laying sod and building benches. He came every day without fail and brought friends to help as well. Grant and I developed a friendship because we spent so much time together. He was very artistic and extremely smart. He had no connection to school. We literally had nothing in common, except that he needed something to do and a place to belong. He loved to serve. It was not the work he loved; it was the connection. When he had an issue come up with grades or a problem at home, his mom would call me directly to see if I could speak with him. I developed many connections with different students through that project. Because I got in over my head with so much labor, I was dependent on the service of students. I had no idea what that would entail, and I would have never taken on such a workload had I realized that amount of physical work would be necessary. I would have also never had the opportunity to develop the relationships with students or discovered that so many students needed that service to connect. I have had many projects at school over the years and there has never been a lack of teachers or students to help serve.

Volunteer service and service learning should play a role in the life of every student. We live in a selfish world and students are extremely self-centered until they are shown how to give to others. Service to others actually improves overall physical and mental health. Serving also adds to life expectancy. People who serve others are generally happier than those who are selfish. Although there is no reward for schools to create service opportunities for students, effective schools realize the benefits for their students and develop a service program. At the National Middle School conference, I discovered several booths dedicated to service. I also learned that companies such as Tom's have attempted to share with students how to give back. Even the local oil company that built the town in which I reside, encourages community service by giving service recipients grant money after a certain amount of hours have been served by their employees.

Our service program is still being built and refined, just like every pure initiative, even after six years. It is a change in culture and must be slowly introduced and encouraged. When starting initiatives and building programs with the purity of intentions to connect with students, it is important to take the needed time to build longevity. I have spent back-to-school-nights introducing the importance of volunteerism to parents. I even challenged the parents to lead the way. We have asked every teacher to provide one service opportunity for students as both an opportunity and example. We have a tiered system of accomplishment for serving up to 5, 10 or 20 hours. In order to keep it on the forefronts of their minds, we recognize students at our weekly celebration, alongside birthdays and shout-outs. We have introduced power points and bulletin boards with service ideas. We have surprise cookouts and extended lunch times for those who have reached at least 5 hours. Our assistant principal even volunteered to spend a day in the school atrium if the students reached a certain amount of volunteer hours. The volunteer sheets came flying in after that proclamation was made.

Since volunteerism is not only a great connection for students, but a healthy lifestyle choice, we want all of our students to participate yearly. National Junior Honor Society captures many students who will connect in other ways, but never serve. In our building NJHS requires at least twenty hours of community service. Those hours are not applicable towards the school service program, but those students will typically start serving in different capacities and continue a lifestyle that gives them the highest tier in the service program as well. At the end of the year we have begun to officially recognize our students during award ceremonies. Although it is not an award, we give them a medal with our school crest and a service symbol to show them that their contribution and effort is recognized as an important accomplishment.

Students who serve others get a sense of accomplishment because it is the first step they take to become a contributing member of society. In every other aspect of their life they are a dependent. Middle school students eat, sleep, drink and go to school on someone else's dime. But when they are able to serve others, they realize the contribution they have made and it gives them a great sense of self-worth. You will see apathetic students take on a new attitude when they have the opportunity to serve others. You will see humility with some students who arrogantly think they hung the moon. Students who come from homes with very little jump at the opportunity to serve others. Serving others changes the individual culture of the environment for each student. A thriving school creates opportunities for students to contribute.

There is a difference between volunteer service and service learning. It can come through varying levels of preparation and professionalism, but service learning is the act of learning a skill or applying knowledge while serving others. For middle schools, it is difficult for students to be exposed to true service learning. Much service learning happens in the form of opportunity where a student is prepared to serve in any capacity. All middle schools can offer opportunities for service learning in the form of painting, minor construction, baking and craft making for others. There are many other opportunities available for each school with the skillset and connectivity of the staff, businesses and parents.

An effective middle school has a service program that encourages and recognizes student service. A majority of staff will offer opportunities for service throughout the year. There will be incentives for involvement for the students and reminders to keep it on their minds. As with any initiative, the school leader must pioneer the efforts and model the direction. If the principals, counselors and teacher leaders show the importance by leading efforts to perform service and provide service opportunities, the teachers and students will embrace the efforts and the benefits.

The last major component of connections is mentoring. Mentoring efforts have been successfully used for generations. It is a matter of organizing the efforts to reach all students. Although efforts have been successful in the past and programs have worked, many schools still hit and miss when it comes to mentoring. If mentoring is a priority, all students will be mentored and have the opportunity to mentor others.

Mentoring comes in so many forms. The most common form of mentoring is adults spending time with the students. It could be a formal one on one or informal as a small group. I received a phone call from a former student asking to be his spiritual advisor. He attended a Catholic school and this was their form of making sure each student had a personal mentor and met regularly. We met monthly over the course of the school year and he kept a journal. Each year our teaching teams meet regularly with a counselor and determine which students need an informal personal mentor. The students may not even realize they have someone watching over them, checking their grades and filling in a parental role where there is nobody else to hold them accountable. Many clubs turn in to an informal group mentoring.

Many students are mentors to younger students. When organized, it can be very effective service learning. We are fortunate to be next door to an elementary school where they have an after school program that offers our students the opportunity to be Hoover Buddies. Our students get to join an after school teacher where they help the teacher by lining up students, playing with students, helping the little ones go to the restroom and reading in small groups. Students learn valuable teaching skills while performing a service for the school. They develop relationships with the elementary students and become invaluable mentors. We have more students sign up than the need dictates.

It is important that there be a mentoring program in place that closes any cracks that students can slip through. The best mentoring program that reached every student and has stood the test of sustainability and continues to positively affect students is found at Thoreau Demonstration Academy. They are a Tribes school and use the Tribal agreements for the basis of their group. Their mentoring group meets for the first twenty minutes each morning. Each teacher is assigned 13-15 students and given curriculum monthly by the counselor. The curriculum is usually based on character traits and many times will be themed by the time of the year. If it is anti-bullying month, curriculum will focus on bullying. If it is African American history month, curriculum will focus on cultural diversity and acceptance. Each morning the students, randomly mixed 6th-8th grade, will sit in a community circle and have their mentoring group. Each group picks their own nickname for the year. The curriculum that day could be questions or it could be an activity. The adult leader has the autonomy to change the conversation. These mentoring groups become a school family. Each family will take on their own personality, but the students become very close. Eighth grade students assume a natural role as the leaders and sixth grade students are generally mentored by the seventh and eighth grade students. If the leader meets daily in community circle and follows the procedures, the mentoring group is successful at reaching all students. Once a week, each group is given the chance to go to intramurals, where they are able to compete as a group or perform team building activities, continuing to solidify the unity of the group. This program has been effective for eighteen years. The teachers see it as a positive experience because they are able to build relationships with students and they understand their role to make sure all students get to talk to an adult. We have created a similar program at Madison Middle School. Bruin Crew has been a smooth initiative because adults in an effective middle school buy in to the opportunity to connect with students. Effective middle schools should reach all students through mentoring. Most students can be affected through multiple avenues of mentoring, but every child should have a school mentor to hold him accountable. The middle school principal must put an emphasis on mentoring before it will be a priority.

After surveying our students, we found that 60% are involved in a club, 15% completed community service, 40% play an instrument and 23% are involved in a school sport. The involvement and offering of all of these opportunities included 96% of the student body. Only 28 students did not have an involvement at school. Those students are now connected through our mentoring program. Even if a student attempts to fall through the crack, we will not let them.

Building student connections and relationships should come naturally for any middle school educator. It must be a mission for a school to affect every student.

Does your school make it a priority to connect to all students? What opportunities do you provide for students to connect?

THIRTEEN

COLLABORATIVE ENVIRONMENT

There is a common perception that teachers like to talk. This perception is only solidified when educators are witnessed in a large group. You can hear them from a great distance. At any education conference, it is impossible to get the whole group to pay attention at one time. Educators are always collaborating. Most of the time, they just cannot shut down their classroom thought processes. Lessons and plans are always unfolding in their minds. Discipline strategies and classroom activities are constantly running through their heads. Educators are expected to collaborate with specific groups on a regular basis.

Effective middle schools have the most collaborative environments of any age group. If a middle school schedule is structured appropriately to meet the teaming needs, middle school teachers will be expected to collaborate daily. They are hired on the premise they will be able to effectively communicate with other adults for the best interest of the students. They are expected to clearly communicate with students. They are also expected to develop relationships with their students. They must be able to speak to parents consistently about student performance and behavior. Middle school teachers must be able to communicate effectively.

Middle school educators are expected to communicate for a purpose. Each meeting will be planned with an outcome that helps the students be more successful. Each meeting has a specific purpose. The amount of time spent collaborating in middle schools separates them from other age groups. It is a natural setup for middle schools to communicate with an objective. Most middle schools build an extra class period in the day just for collaboration. The Dufours, in their infinite wisdom, coined the term *Professional Learning Communities* in their books and articles. There is possibly no greater movement in the history of education than PLC's. The Dufours summed up what effective schools at every grade level do best. They state that schools must simply ask three questions:

"What do we want each student to learn?"
"How will we know when each student has learned it?"
"How will we respond when a student experiences difficulty in learning?"

If schools concentrate on these three questions, they will be successful. It is not a program and it is applicable for all grade levels. If all of the meetings were summed up with student success in mind, there wouldn't be wasted time. Unfortunately, the Dufours made so much sense so quickly to the masses that too many districts have attempted to dilute their movement by pretending to understand and labeling it a program. I am certain that multiple disconnected district leaders have pretended to read their books and demanded the implementation of PLC's. They spent thousands buying everyone a book. A PLC cannot be implemented. You are a PLC or you aren't effective. The Dufours started a movement, not a program. You can be a successful PLC and look different from another PLC experiencing success with the same age group. With that in mind, *an effective middle school is a PLC*. A PLC collaborates for a purpose.

Leaders that expect their teachers to meet regularly

build a collaboration period in the schedule that coincides with the remainder of the teaching team. Ideally, they will have both their plan and collaboration period coincide. Teachers must be given direction and a purpose for each meeting. It is much like building a machine. Once all of the parts are together, you must start the machine and tweak the operation for it to run properly. When everything is running properly, it runs on its own without micromanagement, because it runs smoothly. There are several meetings that are integral in our operation for student success as an effective middle school. Some effective middle schools call their meetings by a different name, but the purpose of the collaborative sessions must be included if your school is successfully reaching all students.

The **team meeting** is when each grade level teaching team collaborates for the purpose of establishing common procedures, integration of curriculum, and sharing calendar events to flex their schedule. These meetings can last a few minutes or an hour. They may stretch until the next day, depending on whether they have completed their task. They should meet regularly. At the beginning of the year, they will meet extensively to make their classroom procedures uniform for each class. This practice has proven invaluable for new teachers. Team members continue to collaborate throughout the year about procedures as needed.

The team members work to integrate curriculum during their team meeting. When students make connections with each discipline, they are more likely to remember what they have learned. This is an ongoing process and teachers who have not been exposed to integration will need examples. If most teachers were honest, they would not be able to tell you what is going on outside of their discipline. They have no clue about the objectives being covered in any other core class. When teachers sit together and share their lesson plans, it is amazing how they can integrate the curriculum. Teachers must be afforded the time and the directed expectation from their building leader before integration will be a priority.

Also during team meetings, if the schedule allows for

teams to be flexible to maximize instructional time, teams should use this time to review any calendar events in which to avoid days with minimal instruction. Quite typically, if a teacher is only going to see three of their four core classes, they will likely use the day to enrich the three classes instead of getting behind in their fourth class by introducing new material. If a schedule is flexible, they can use this time to divide their three periods in to four and introduce new lesson plans with shorter class periods. This is a simple concept that must be utilized whenever possible to avoid wasting the time of our students. Team meetings are also the time teachers will coordinate remedial efforts with students who are being called in for remediation on a daily basis. Student time will need to be shared and students will also need to miss minimal time from their elective classes. Teachers can coordinate this during their team meeting.

A **thumbs meeting** must be held every two weeks. Some schools call it **kid talk**. The name doesn't hold meaning; the results make it successful. Teachers collaborate and bring personal knowledge of each student. Teachers meet as a team with a counselor and administrator when available to name every student on their roster. It is essential every name is read and the group is given the opportunity to collaborate if needed. As the counselor or teacher leader reads through each name, anyone can say yes and the students' name is highlighted. When they are finished reading all of the names, the team will go through the list of highlighted students to discuss any concerns. Team members will discuss meeting student learning styles, classroom discipline and knowledge of personal issues that might affect their education. They will go to all lengths to discuss strategies to make their students successful. It could be that grades are dropping, attendance has been an issue, or they cannot stay in their seat. Counselors can bring an insight if they have knowledge of relevant information.

There are times when a student has a newly broken home, a tragedy has stricken their family, a relative or friend has been diagnosed with a disease, or something awful has happened that they haven't shared with each teacher. It could be a social issue, such as a boyfriend, girlfriend, or intimidation that has them acting weird. The thumbs meeting is the time to bring these issues to light to collaborate on successful strategies to minimize the distraction. I have seen light bulbs go off in the head of a teacher when they find out that a child is going through a rough time. They realize why that student is distant, distracted, or even seemingly disrespectful. A new level of patience will suddenly be bestowed upon a child who was thought to be rude just moments before because vital information was shared. There are strategies each teacher will use with their students that can become team knowledge if successful. A thumbs meeting can save students by giving all teachers relevant information to make them successful. A thumbs meeting is never to be negative about students, it is only to share information to make teachers stronger.

During my second year of teaching, a girl named Kolby walked up and said, "You need to talk to Jamie." They were friends, and I wasn't sure if she was just kidding. Jamie is still one of my favorite students of all time, even though I haven't seen him in over a decade. He had a care and compassion about him that is rare. He was also a big football player that eventually played on the line for a state championship in high school. He was a unique and rare student who had the respect of everyone, including students, teachers and other parents. I counted myself fortunate to know Jamie very well as a teacher and his coach. As students entered the class I saw Jamie with a rare pose, his head down, as he entered the room. I asked him to step aside while I greeted the others. As the class got started with the daily prompt, I asked him in the hall what was wrong. He immediately got defensive, as if I didn't care. It was so strange to see him act this way. If he had spoken to me or any other teacher the way he was talking, he would have been in the office in trouble under normal circumstances. After a few more hateful remarks, Jamie finally told me that his dad left his mom. He even stated it hatefully. I reached up and gave him a hug. He broke down immediately and cried. Jamie and I came from very different cultures, but we shared an appreciation for our differences and common ground in our beliefs. We stayed out in the hall for a while and talked about it. With Jamie's permission, I immediately got on the horn with his other teachers and informed them of his situation. I didn't give all of the details, but I made sure his attitude didn't get him in trouble with anyone else. That is the only time I had ever seen that young man distraught. If I had not been trained to communicate with other team members, and we were not all on the same page with confidential information, Jamie would have been in trouble that day. He would have missed out on football and his grades would have suffered. He would have probably been in trouble at home as well. The dominoes can keep tumbling when a middle school student is falling apart. Fortunately, that was not the case with Jamie. Communication is key to the teaching team.

Grade level discipline teams formally meet weekly, but informally meet daily, to harness the best teaching strategies to reach all students. Depending on the flavor of the year for programs, these can be called data meetings, grade level department meetings, or a host of other names. The objective is the same, to put as many minds together and share strategies for instructing students. It is no secret to educators that the lesson they thought all students should have learned might not have actually reached the students. Learning styles are consistently changing and teachers must stay abreast of new strategies to reach students. Available data must be used to give relevance to the collaboration. Official data through pre testing, post testing, goal setting and evaluating learning strategies can be extremely helpful. Unofficially discussing student involvement and performance is more often the scenario and much more efficient. Individual students who did not learn the objective are identified and remediated. Teachers must use common assessments to truly be effective in collaborating for effective strategies.

Effective middle schools also collaborate as a **department** on a regular basis. A monthly meeting to determine curriculum alignment is usually sufficient. The purpose of a full department meeting is to vertically align the curriculum and discuss department needs. Vertical curriculum alignment is crucial for teachers to cover the appropriate material to prepare their students for the next school year, especially when standards are changing.

If there is a student whom teachers, counselors or parents believe should be on an **Individual Education Plan**, teaching teams meet as needed. They assess the student over a period of time and make the determination from the results of the data if the student needs an IEP and what the IEP will include. Teachers will also meet on **504** plans if parents have requested one or if teachers have proposed the need for one to meet student needs.

Each official meeting is for a purpose. An effective middle school understands their purpose and takes pride in meeting the needs of their students. Teachers can explain why they collaborate and how it benefits students. This is by no means an exhaustive list of meetings for a purpose, just the essential needs for collaboration that define success for middle school students. In order for a teacher to be able to collaborate with a team, they must be able to actually get along with the other team members. As an adult, that concept would seem to be understood. Not only must a middle school teacher work with the toughest age group, they must also get along with every adult in the building. That is usually a very eccentric group of people. The stronger the working relationship with the other team members, the more likely individual student interest will be best served.

I have been a witness to a teacher who can differentiate the curriculum and develop student relationships but cannot get along with other teachers. Obviously, the most important element is the classroom. Unfortunately, the entire team begins to lose function and becomes stagnant. Student best interest will be lost on a team that does not function and collaborate on a regular basis. I have also seen teachers who are comfortable in front of the classroom, but have anxiety issues when talking to others in the hallway. If a teacher cannot communicate freely with other adults and make conversation productive through the collaborative structure of the environment, they do not need to teach in a middle school. Middle school teachers have to work together. Their relationship with one another is the stopgap. They must possess a personality to be able to get along with other professionals. When a teacher accepts the position, they agree to work in a collaborative environment. Although some teachers may find success with a different age group, middle school might not be an option because they are not riding solo. It is okay to work alone and do a great job, just not in a middle school.

If a team is not meeting on a regular basis for any of the scheduled collaborative meetings, they will not be successful. Teachers who are accustomed to success, expect their teammates to be strong. If they are not strong, the weakness will reflect in the behavior of all of their students. If procedures are weak in one teacher's classroom, it will trickle in to the next classroom. If teachers are not collaborating about students, there will be missed opportunities to meet learning styles. Teachers will also not be made privy to situations that could merit an extra level of patience for a student having a difficult time. If someone is not working to flex the schedule, there will be wasted instructional hours. If there is a weak link in the team, it is noted and brought to the attention of the principal.

When a middle school team is functioning at a high level, it is because they are able to collaborate effectively. The collaboration is the reason for the success. When teachers realize their success, they take a level of pride in meeting the needs of the students. It is incredible to see the transformation when the needs of all students are met. If teachers have ever been in a sinking ship with a school that treads water constantly and depends on a few individuals to keep them afloat, it is a relief to be in a school that cruises successfully. A place where each person can play a part in operating an effective team.

In order for the teaming concept to be initiated, there must be strong leadership. The school leader must spell out the purpose and direction of each meeting. He must also join all of the meetings in the beginning, so each gathering will go in the right direction. The building leader must also periodically check in to make sure that healthy collaboration is taking place on a regular basis. The principal of the school must wisely discern if they are going to keep teachers who are struggling in their relationships with other staff members. Although it is a difficult decision, student progress has to be the factor in making those decisions. Middle schools must have strong leadership in place in order for teachers to understand the purpose.

It is amazing how teachers will take over when they understand the purpose. When the nature of each meeting is comprehended and it becomes part of the culture, there is no need to micromanage or even check up on most teaching teams. Even when there are cuts to the budget and teaming is compromised, teachers will still find a way to collaborate, despite the setback, because they believe in their mission.

Can you work on a team for the purpose of students? Can you collaborate with others on a daily basis? Do you enjoy being a major factor in the success of all students?

FOURTEEN
EFFECTIVE USE OF DATA

The use of data has become the key topic in most schools and the driving force behind most decision making in education and the workforce. The term data-driven has become a badge many educators like to wear as a description of their leadership. Most school districts have completed multiple book studies on data. Teachers are put on teams to study every minutia of data available. There is a belief that data has the answers to make an entire population successful. This chapter will fly in the face of many followers of such beliefs, but please read it in its entirety. Data has many uses.

Schools leaders should only wear the badge of student-driven. All decisions should be made in the best interest of each individual student, only using data as a tool. An effective middle school focuses on the individual student. It is extremely important to attain valid data. Student academic data is a measurement of a child's knowledge at a moment in time.

In order to gain a perspective on the use of test scores and the data that it provides, we must look at the history of such testing. After the short history lesson on the use of data in the past thirty years, I will address proper use of data in today's environment.

In the 80's, students took state tests one day a year. Students were given all tests on the same day because educators were focused on teaching important curriculum and they viewed this day as a waste of time. Testing was a nuisance. Results were typically given for a class, but not too many people paid attention because nobody knew when they would receive them. Most parents never even saw their children's score. At that time classroom grades were the driving force and all the data a parent needed to know. Parents didn't know their student was making a bad grade till progress reports every four and a half weeks. There was a need for standardized testing to become more relevant.

In the 90's, the results from the test scores would arrive around December from the previous testing cycle. Someone would bring them down to the classroom and a huge stack of data would sit on a table as the teacher would leisurely go through the numbers marveling at the students who graced their classroom just 7 months ago. It was the equivalent of four reams of paper stacked all in one pile. Teachers may have noted some problems with certain objectives if they could decipher the spreadsheets. It is actually possible that they had already covered the failed topics again before they knew the students failed the year before, rendering the data useless. Most of the time, the objectives teachers were supposed to teach were not released until February, so they were working off the previous year's objectives. Teachers were already in the heart of the school year and too busy to worry about last year. The scores from the current students would belong to their former teacher. Teachers gave the same amount of respect to the method as the level of common sense the whole system made. There was not any level of accountability because there wasn't any direction. Math and reading teachers knew who were proficient very quickly, because they used their own classroom assessments.

In the early 2000's, when educators realized No Child Left Behind would seriously affect their lives, scores became more important. Educators would get the previous year's test results two days before school started if they were lucky and pilfer through the scores to determine which students needed help. A rush copy of the student scores were sent to their former and current teacher. They were given opportunities to show proficiency and moved forward if they were able to prove that they understood objectives. Attention was given to overall class performance in math and reading. The students' previous teachers would try to see if their scores were equal to or better than last year. Teachers moved forward with the school year in hopes that their scores would be better than the previous year. NCLB still made the mistake of comparing last year's students to the current students, which every educator in America knows is completely ridiculous.

In today's environment, our students will test and memorize their number of correct to see if they passed, because they are so anxious. Some students will even get nauseous before taking the state test. Tests are online, so they will know the results immediately. They believe it is a measure of what their future holds. Hopefully the computer servers won't crash as in previous years. Teachers will compile the numbers and wait for the unofficial results in a couple of weeks. They will then be able to break down by each objective what students missed. Some students are bad test takers, but that is not shown in the numbers. A few of the students are apathetic and will not try on the test, but they will be treated as if they haven't learned all year. Some kids eat breakfast; some do not. Some are moody; some got in a fight with a parent, and some just broke up with a girlfriend. Teachers are a wreck during testing because they are hoping all variables line up for their students to show their personal best on the exam. They are hoping for great increases. They know they will have just a short time to enjoy their student's successes before they have to start stressing about the next group they have yet to meet. Those scores will be arriving soon.

Most people are in agreement that testing has become too intense, specifically all of the teachers, students and parents involved. Basically every stakeholder believes we are not going in the right direction by testing constantly. Leave it to education to let the pendulum swing too far. The purpose for data should be to improve instruction. We have become so data-driven at a national level, that we are missing the purpose. We are dealing with individual adolescent performance. Good luck to anyone who ever thinks that will be a perfect science.

There are individuals and companies that believe they have the answer for all student learning and success. They declare they have student learning down to a science. There are companies that will claim multiple level advances for every student if you just buy their program. Companies present data to show an imaginary perfect science to instructing all students. Some speakers and consultants will tell you of their success and show you data to support their claims. There are now online schools declaring they have the answer for all students. If you are able to buy their program, your students will advance in math and reading. By the way, those companies and schools make a profit. All of them have students who use their curriculum and yet, there are no perfect middle school test scores. Although the companies claim to know the answers, they cannot produce perfect results.

There is data that shows if every student were able to get a certain teacher, that would make them successful, because the teacher yields great results. Data shows an effective teacher can advance students 2 years, while an ineffective teacher will leave students years behind. If every student could have Mrs. Van for eighth grade English, all students would be able to read and write. If we could only do a study and pick out the qualities that should be evident in all teachers, we can list those qualities and put a rating system next to the teacher to see if they measure up and perform. We can even put their students' results up next to their name to give them an incentive to make sure they can learn. This will solve everything by putting numbers to the equation. Then, of course, all schools will be successful. This has been implemented, and there are no perfect middle school test scores. Not one school can boast perfect results.

Everything depends on great leadership. Data shows if leadership is strong, all students will be successful. If we could just put a list of qualities and ratings for every great leader and only hire and keep principals, headmasters, and deans who met those qualities, the students' needs would be met. We would have infallible schools and all students would learn. Teachers would be held to high standards and every classroom would yield perfect results. Yet, there are stringent and impossible measurements of leadership in place. There are companies banking on their tools of measurement that they have sold states and districts at a premium, to hold all leadership to the fire. Again, there are no perfect middle school test scores.

It is an amazing declaration in education that there is data to show success for all people in all places at all times. There are many people who claim to have the answers to reach all students, but nobody can claim they have reached an entire city, state, or nation. There is not data available to show that if you implement a specific program, all students will be able to read or pass an algebra test. No leader can claim that all students will pass a test if they attend their school. There isn't an online school that can show that all students will be able to pass a test through their program. There isn't any perfection in education. Billions of dollars spent, but the results are the same. There are a few that have done a remarkable job of reaching a school, but it is limited to a site and a time. And again, there is not any school with perfect test scores.

We are dealing with humans. Data can be useful, but it will not be scientifically perfect when dealing with students. It is impossible for number crunchers who couldn't lead a classroom to claim what should be taught and how it should be taught in each classroom. They cannot fathom the responsibility in a lab. Data is great when you connect it to each child. All data must be understood to be useful. There is no perfect data in education. All data is fallible. It does not matter how long a study lasts, it isn't long enough to understand the variables in the life of a child.

Certain qualities of data must be in place to render it effective.

Data must be timely. Teachers in an effective school collect data daily. Unbeknownst to the outside world, effective teachers have been collecting data on a daily basis for years. This is in the form of official and unofficial assessments. Teachers need to know if their instruction is effective. They need a quick turnaround. They will usually know by a quiz or test. Some teachers can see it in the feedback from an activity, depending on the subject. They will generally reteach a concept if the students do not understand it through an assessment. If it is a standardized test, the results must come back before the students move on to another objective. With state testing, results need to come back to the teacher well in advance of the new school year for it to be used for the next year. Teachers need time to disaggregate the data and adjust lessons if they realize they have failed in an area.

Data must be valid. Teachers need to see data that is untainted or biased. One of the most irritating parts of education is dissecting data that is not even valid. When a score comes back that a child cannot read, but they have test anxiety and you can bear witness of their reading abilities, it is not valid data. If the powers that be decide to change the cut score of a test, or change the rigor of the assessment, it renders the test invalid when comparing to previous years' results. When the teachers later find out that a test changed to cover objectives they were not made aware to prepare their students, it will not be valid. Educators treasure valid data because it can be used to improve instruction or help individual students.

Data must be limited. In order for data to be used effectively, it must come in small waves. It must be limited to be useful. The whole purpose of data is to use it to improve instruction. Students learn small portions of information at a time. An annual test can measure that moment in time, but should not be used to determine if a student learned that school year. Again, the common sense factor lets everyone know when too much time has been spent in the lab. A teacher can determine if a student learned a concept every couple of weeks. The student's grade should reflect if they have learned during the school year.

What is too much data? There is too much data collection when the people who make a difference with the data are not able to use it. Students are over evaluated. One eighth grade teacher documented over 100 mandated district, state and national tests. There is no possible way to use the data, so why collect it in the first place? That is a waste of instructional time. Even if a teacher were able to use the data, is it effective to eliminate hands-on learning activities because they are busy administering tests? Testing, quizzing and prepping for testing and quizzing takes time. Most students nationwide are in school a total of 185 days. Should they be tested over half of those days? The answer is absolutely not. Teachers will not be able to remediate because their students have another test to take. Obviously, our focus should be on the students. Very few educators got in to education so they could pour over spreadsheets provided for them by a principal, education service center, or the state department. The individual student is the reason they answered the call to teach.

How should state testing data be used? Students should be formally evaluated every year. This gives the parent and teacher an idea of their progress, but not a scientifically exact number on their ability. Teachers should receive the scores well in advance of the next school year. When teachers receive their booklets of test scores, they will break down the students score by objective and list their individual performance from weak to strong. Students will be remediated if they did not pass the state test. An effective middle school will use guided study, built in to their elective schedule. Guided study is when a teacher calls a student out of elective class to remediate a concept the student did not understand in class or on the state test. They also use guided study if the students do not understand a current concept or are failing a class. This is also revealed in assessments, both formal and informal during the school year. Students will be formally and informally tested on a consistent basis that does not interrupt the flow of lessons that enrich a classroom.

Each time a student is tested, quizzed or surveyed, the results should be used for student remediation or teacher evaluation of methods. Individually, if students did not understand a concept, they need to be remediated. If a majority of students failed an objective on a standardized test or if the majority of students failed a class test, the teacher will realize she did not reach the students with her teaching methods. It is the teacher's responsibility to improve her method of instruction. Teachers are aware they can always improve on instruction; it is part of their intrinsic motivation to improve.

Beyond those reasons, students should be busy learning in their classrooms. Testing is not learning, testing is evaluating.

What data do we use? All data should be used by teachers who deem it appropriate. Teachers are educated individuals who consider their jobs integral to the success of students. If they have all data at their fingertips in a timely manner, they will be able to make the determination of need for each student. Teachers give quizzes and tests frequently and use the data appropriately. Teachers should also make the administration, parents, and the public aware of unnecessary testing for their students. There have been multiple reports of testing for compilation of information that goes directly to testing companies for results where they sell their information. It is not acceptable for anyone outside of education to make a profit from adolescents. Valid data should be disaggregated for the benefit of each student. If we are not using the results of quizzes, tests or surveys, they should never be administered. When data is timely, valid, and limited, teachers are able to use the data to improve instruction. When teachers can improve their instruction, they can reach more students.

It's all about the student. There is not a teacher in the profession who had a desire to reach a higher number on their percentages on state testing for their goals as a young professional. Teachers are leaving the profession quicker than the colleges can replace them for that reason. Teachers wish to reach every student, but do not care if someone holds their feet to the fire for a number. There is a better, more lucrative job in the future if a teacher chooses. Teachers entered the profession to reach students, but the action of attaching a number has deflated the efforts of accepting the call to teach. Data is important but should not deflate the efforts of the individuals who care enough to put themselves in harm's way to reach tomorrow's leaders.

The entire purpose of data must be to concentrate on the individual student. Every student is important, not as a percentage, but as an individual. Teachers want to reach each student because they are important as individuals. Students are never a number to teachers, they are only a number to those who do not know their name. The success of students is the entire purpose for any person who enters the profession of education.

The majority of people do not care about a number, they care about people. It is not possible to perfect the delivery and connection of every individual to the successful components of education by just collecting the right data. Teachers shoulder the accountability to reach every student academically. It is the responsibility of every teacher to make sure that every attempt has been made to educate all students.

At the end of the day, parents and educators want students to learn. They want students to grow and flourish. Placing a number on a child and determining their abilities is criminal. Data should be collected and used to help individual students. Data should only be shared with the parties that positively affect the child.

I recently visited a highly effective school that has maintained the same administration and initiatives for almost 20 years. I spoke with their principal about testing and the use of data. He has thousands of educators visit his school yearly to glean their approach to education, since they have been so successful with a diverse group of students. He is ready to show spreadsheets of student growth. He believes in the mission of his school and he has the data to prove their effectiveness. He looked at me and said, "If we are doing the right things, the data will show it." He went on to say, "You cannot worry about test scores, you have to focus on students." I am certain it cannot be said any better.

An effective middle school that thrives will review and disaggregate all applicable data to improve instruction and student learning. Targeting instruction will be intentional. Teachers will also diversify to seek every other available source of assessments, both formal and informal, for opportunities to enrich curriculum so students will thrive. Effective middle schools are student driven, using data as a tool.

Can you assess a student and come to a conclusion they understand what you taught? Can you focus on individual student comprehension? Can you collaborate with others to see why their instruction was more effective? Can you determine the validity of a test score? Can you stand up and say no when data is not student driven?

FIFTEEN

MIDDLE SCHOOL SUPPORTS

An effective school has many support systems that help students and teachers. Supports range from academic, social, emotional and psychological. Some are a safety net so students do not fall through the cracks. Some supports are for teachers who need all the tools available to reach students. In a middle school, the depth of support never seems sufficient because we are dealing with a diverse group of needy students. There are support systems for teachers, students, and the school. The following are supports that an effective middle school should have in place. Without these, schools cannot function properly.

Teacher Supports

If there is anything that can make good people lose their religion, it is technology. I have seen technology fail and panic set in for poor individuals whose dependency was too great on their electronic creation. The beads of sweat will begin to emerge on their brow when they realize they will have to punt for the entire day because the infrastructure has failed on the device they planned to use for the lesson. There are districts and schools that are very technologically driven. The latest and greatest that a grant and bond can provide will be at the fingertips of every teacher and student. When they go to use the devices, there has to be support personnel to help open doors for teachers to get maximum use out of the investment.

Some districts are technology ignorant. There is technology that goes unused because nobody can figure out how to get it operational. They receive federal or bond monies and spend it in a hurry. Someone puts it in a closet and it sits. There have been boxes of brand new technology items tossed in the trash because it became obsolete before it was opened.

Some districts are technology poor. They do not have leadership that drives the cause to communicate and reach students. This includes communication inside and outside of the classroom. They have some equipment and the teachers seek to reach students through every means possible. There are teachers who operate under stringent control of a tech department that doesn't understand teacher needs. Teachers figure out a way around so they can reach their students. They have a technology department that throws roadblocks up to teachers and stifles creativity in the name of safety. There is no excuse for leaders to drag their feet in technology. These districts should have their leader replaced with someone who can still relate to a classroom. Technology is that important.

There are districts who support technology and maximize the potential to reach students both inside and outside of the classroom. District leadership encourages technology departments to listen to classroom teacher needs. Valuable web sites are supported and apps are available. Students will be reached by whatever means possible. Teachers do not feel a level of frustration, but a level of support that encourages creativity. This is how every district should operate. It allows for an effective school.

One of the greatest decisions that must be made when a new teacher enters the building is who will be the mentor teacher. Speaking from experience, there is a potential for the mentor teacher to have a great impact on the new teacher. A teacher fresh out of college needs every support afforded. The mentor teacher should be the best teacher in the building. Although students have been trained in college, when they enter that classroom for the first time, a new teacher needs the daily support from the most competent teacher. When a medical student leaves the classroom and enters their residency, they want to study with the best surgeon. They want the doctor who has the greatest success rate. While training to do surgery, everyone can agree she needs to be trained by the most competent surgeon in the field. That is the doctor we want to perform our surgery. The same is true for teachers; we want them to be trained by the best in the field. There are teachers who have had success reaching all students by methods the new teacher might have never been exposed. New methods are created daily that colleges may not have grasped and implemented in to their curriculum. A great mentor will spend an extensive amount of time making sure their protégé is competent. A few years ago I hired a great teacher candidate. Although I knew she was a good candidate, she still needed to have someone train her in the position. Mrs. McKinney was a master teacher in the building and the perfect candidate for mentor. I even had Mrs. McKinney officially interview the candidate with the team. Their relationship is still strong and she is considered the reason for this teachers' ability to reach students as a reading teacher. Mrs. McKinney informed me later that year she was a little bit hurt that I did not consider her for another position in the building when it had opened. I told her that the most important position for her was the mentoring of a great young teacher. She reluctantly agreed because she understood the effect she had on the new teacher. Mrs. McKinney is the best and the most important position for her that year was is in the classroom training a new teacher. The best mentors tend to take ownership of new teachers, not allowing them to falter and communicating all needs to the building principal. An effective school has leadership who values the mentor and places new teachers with the most successful teachers in the building.

A school that values quality in the classroom encourages and provides professional development for all of their teachers. Although many educators would rather have a root canal than be sent to training for a day, school systems that have actual professional development on a consistent basis have successful classrooms. There are multiple forms of professional development. There are school wide programs and content specific professional development. School wide programs get everyone on the same page and allow for common language across the disciplines. Most will be character education and classroom management and each school district should have adopted their own. School wide professional development should be limited to allow for content specific training. Content-specific PD should be supported and encouraged by the school so teachers can enrich their area of expertise and stay excited to deliver content to the students.

Some districts afford an instructional coach. An instructional coach will work with all teachers to provide professional development as needed. The teacher who serves in this role can be highly effective if she has the respect of the entire staff. She is never an evaluator or teachers will feel uncomfortable asking for her expertise. The instructional coach must work very closely with the principal to determine overall staff development needs. The coach will also provide in-house staff training. The instructional coach is instrumental in helping new teachers during the first few weeks of school, frequently visiting classrooms and offering support. She will continue to support them throughout the school year. The coach will also offer lesson plans supporting the differentiation of instruction, giving multiple examples upon request. Veteran teachers must feel comfortable asking the instructional coach for support as needed. The coach must have very good relationships with the entire staff. The instructional coach will work with outside consultants for the implementation of district wide programs. She will also collaborate with administration to provide staff development for school initiatives to help successfully implement them to the school site.

The middle school teaching team is the greatest support for teachers in the middle. The teaching team is meant to be a support for each member. When there is a parent meeting, the team meets together with the parent because they each share the same group of children. Teachers can collaborate with parents for academic or behavior patterns. If a teacher has struggles with student discipline, classroom procedures or curriculum differentiation, he will discover support in his team meetings. When a team is cohesive, it makes it difficult for any teacher to fail. The team should be a strong support for their colleagues. If a teacher is struggling, all of their students are struggling as well.

Student Supports

Student supports do not replace the struggle. The struggles from the deficiencies in this life help us build strength and resilience. The greatest stories of triumph and inexplicable strength are due to the struggles for survival and success. Grit is developed when people struggle for success and will not accept failure. As a person achieves success, his confidence grows and failure ceases to be an option. Student supports should never serve to be an enabling system. Support systems should encourage and fill in the gaps for students who are missing major elements that present a deficiency too large for them to overcome. It takes discernment to judge the difference between a struggle and an unattainable deficiency. When there is something missing, deficient or damaged in the life of a child, whether it be a learning disability, a social problem or familial neglect, the school will try to bridge that gap for the student to be successful in learning.

There are a handful of supports for students in every middle school. The caliber that these supports are functioning will determine if students are receiving the best option from the adults. Just having a program in place is not enough to merit the distinction of a great job supporting students. Just as in any program or position, the leadership will need to determine and hold accountable any support systems a school claims to possess to help their students.

The first line of support that has helped millions of students to bridge the gap in learning deficiencies is special education. I have known two great special education teachers in my career. I've known many more that do a good job, but Pam and Morgan continue to make an undeniable impact that changes student lives. They are truly called to teach students with disabilities. If the special education department functions, the entire school is positively affected. Conversely, if the special education department struggles with incompetency, the entire school is negatively affected.

I met Pam the day I was introduced to be a teacher. It was my first day on the job and she was there to greet and grill me. I wasn't even on contract yet. She wanted to know everything about me. Pam has no problem letting you know that she was a special education student. She will also tell you her accomplishments, including a master's degree, because she believes all special education students can be successful. Pam will talk ninety miles a minute but she is feeling you out at the same time. She wants to know who she can trust with her students. She places each one of her students with the teachers she believes will have the greatest impact. She splits them up and places them by their personalities and the teachers' strengths. You know after spending a few moments with Pam that she loves her students. She talks with a level of excitement about each child. Success is the only option for her students. Pam introduced me to special education. Through all of my schooling and internships, I did not realize the purpose. She showed me that her students could learn and that just because they had a disability, they were no less intelligent than any other student. They had a deficiency and we were there to make sure that deficiency was rectified. I have since realized what a blessing it was to have Pam as my first special education teacher. She didn't care if you thought she was crazy. She made sure you understood each child she placed in your classroom and more importantly worked with each child to help them be successful. She would join in lessons and help all students learn. The regular education students didn't even know she was a special education teacher. They received help from her when they asked. Pam does not care about your opinion of her, she wants to make sure you take special care of the students she is called to teach.

Morgan has an incredible relationship with each student. She spends the majority of her day helping students with emotional issues and will not take a regular education job even when offered. She co-teaches with several teachers. Morgan will make sure you understand each child. She calmly communicates to teachers and administrators until they understand the students. She can come up with analogies to describe what the students are thinking or why they react the way they do. She will make you see the actions of the child through their eyes. She assists teachers with strategies for reaching those students academically. The assistance to administration to help with student disciplinary measures helps each student individually because her relationships are strong enough to determine what will work to change their behavior. Morgan is gifted with a calmness in any situation. She is faced with students and teachers who are not calm when her assistance is needed. She can bring the correct answer to the situation in a very soothing manner. A great special education teacher is not always the norm, just as an effective middle school is not always the norm. Society is forever in debt to a person who has accepted the call to teach special education and fulfills their duties.

One of the first faces most people see when they enroll a student is the counselor. The role of the counselor is complex. They are the guidance counselor, enrollment coordinator, testing coordinator and the grade level counselor for students. They are also drama, bully and mood swing specialists. They entered the profession to help students through this time of their life. If they are any good, they hate testing because it takes away from their time to visit with students. They are the first line of support with student social issues and drama. They assist students who will never come talk with an administrator. They help students in groups with problems and they talk to students individually. By nature of their call, they never turn a child away. They come to every thumbs meeting with teaching teams so they can contribute and understand all of the behavioral issues with their assigned students. Some students will ask to see them when they are not their assigned counselor and they always oblige. Much of their impact is not measureable because it is dealing with personal problems. Counselors spend a great amount of time with parents as well, acclimating them to their children's new found behavior patterns. Many children should thank a counselor for the advice they have given their parents. In an effective school, counselors are never used for discipline because their students will see them differently. If a counselor is a disciplinarian, the children may not trust them with vital information. Every student and family in the building is positively effected when there is good counselor support.

An effective middle school has many programs and systems in place designed to make sure every student connects. A fine arts program with band, orchestra and choir. An athletic program that offers a broad range of sports to students. An array of clubs that attract special interest. A community service program designed to bridge in to service learning and connect to students. A mentoring program that connects every student with an adult. If a student is connected in some way to school, they will feel supported. Providing student connections is the greatest support system in the school.

Another level of support that was mentioned in earlier chapters is remediation. All students should be remediated when they are unable to master a concept. Many students just need extra support to be able to understand. Remediation can be through guided study classes, lunch or after school tutoring. The entire purpose for a student to attend school is learning. If the student is not learning, they need extra support to help.

Although all of these supports are in place, there are still some who need a level of attention that is beyond what they will receive in a normal school setting. Some students have social and emotional issues that will inhibit them from being successful. *Schools who are focused on all students have an alternative education program in place to help students who need a smaller setting and online schooling with an ability to spend more time with the students.* An alternative education program will allow students with emotional and social issues the ability to go to school and receive normal credits. This is an essential support for any school.

An effective school will do everything to lend every support to students. No student should fall through the cracks. Some students will still be apathetic to all resources afforded to them. There are very few that choose to be unsuccessful, but it should not ever be because the school has failed to reach them. Effective schools exhaust every available resource to help each child be successful.

The greatest support a student can receive is from family. Nothing can replace parental support. Students with a supportive family have a better support system at home to keep them accountable than students who come from homes with no expectations or accountability. The constant decline in family unity has resulted in more students without their needs being met. In some cases, teachers and counselors have filled the role of missing parents.

As stated previously, every position outside of the classroom is support personnel for the classroom. There must be a culture that the entire purpose for a school including the office, cafeteria, janitorial crew, bus driver and the education service center is for what happens in that classroom. Everything should serve to support the classroom.

A student should be met with a warm greeting from a kind bus driver who knows their name. A feeling of safety and care should encompass that oversized yellow box as it transports our students. The person in control of that culture is the driver. They could be the difference between students learning or being distracted all day by what happened on the bus.

The cafeteria personnel interact with most students every day. What they put on the menu can make an impact on student learning and behavior. The manner in which they treat and educate the students can make a difference in the attitude and diets of the students as they return to class. Their support of the classroom is more than just the veggies they serve.

A good portion of the janitorial crew does not ever see students. Their impact is enormous. *The level of pride and safety that a clean building can provide is underappreciated when they are doing a good job.* The vandalism, bugs, and general feeling of disgust is what will happen when a building does not get cleaned. Their support is also more than just trash liners and Windex. They are an essential element to a successful school.

The education service center, the main offices of the superintendent and his staff, exist entirely to support the classroom. Most superintendents in districts with a sizeable amount of students do not have much contact with the classroom. Their job is policy, bonds, and grants. They deal with angry parents, security and board members. They earn their salary in education, but not dealing with students. Their job is to support the classroom; in every decision they make. There are leaders who just want their name on the news and the sides of buildings while they build a political career, but at the end of the day, their responsibility is to protect and provide for the students learning in the classroom. Effective superintendents, board members and directors spend a considerable amount of time visiting schools to understand and support the needs of the classroom.

Do you understand the reason for supports? Have you seen a child try to fall through the cracks? Can you appreciate the level of importance that all aspects of the school can play in the life of a child?

THE CONCLUSION

Middle school students in every town and state deserve teachers, classrooms, and schools that are highly effective. This age group is no longer the forgotten middle child. There must be a special focus to place our students in thriving environments. Our students are that important. We have the knowledge and the ability to create environments conducive to make this crazy time of their life a positive experience.

Teachers should be called to their positions. They should possess impeccable character and an uncanny desire to reach every student. Their classrooms should be a safe place, embracing structured freedom that engages all students in an amazing learning environment.

Our schools must be equipped with a visionary leader who understands and relates to this age group and the structures of a middle school. Schools must thrive through a welcoming, friendly and safe environment. They should have flexible scheduling so teachers can remediate and collaborate. They must connect to every student and use data to target instruction for individual students. Every child and community should take pride in their middle school because they meet the needs of the children and families of the community.

If you are at this point in the book, I must thank you for multiple reasons. First of all, you have finished the book, which I do appreciate. More importantly, if you have made it this far, you are an educator. You are a middle level educator. You have been gifted for the toughest group to teach. You love your students and you desire with all of your being for them to be successful in life. Thank you. The purpose of this information is to encourage and give a direction to those who are in the trenches with students every day.

You should be able to recognize an effective middle school that is thriving. If you are a prospective college student in search of your first employment, you should now recognize a thriving middle school. You now know what you must demand to observe in order to accept employment in a school. Your efforts should never be in vain and the general public needs longevity out of your career. Only accept a position that resembles an environment and structure you have read in the previous chapters. Ask questions during your interview that pertain to the non-negotiable elements of a middle school.

Thank you for answering the call to teach middle school. Many people float through this life and only see their own small world. You have accepted one of the toughest responsibilities. Your world is inclusive of your students and the burden of their safety and success. You said yes. You have the gifts to make your students feel safe and confident in their education.

Thank you for the nights and weekends you have sacrificed in lieu of grading. The knowledge that the students would need their paper back as feedback for tomorrow's assignment propelled you to pull an all-nighter. Thank you for putting the same effort in to grading as the students have in to completing their assignment. They do notice. Thank you for not paying quite as much attention to the movie you rented because the student essay was a little more interesting. Thank you for sacrificing all of your "free time" to make sure your students received timely information.

Thank you for the many games you have attended. I am sure you really appreciated that farmer's tan you received right after school at the softball game. I am certain that you preferred the football game over a night out on the town. Every year, you have attended games for students. You could have probably had a nest egg with all of the money you have spent at the snack shack over the years. The importance level the students have felt when you attend their games has made them feel special. Thank you for the activities you have attended. You put a smile on the face of a child when they noticed you were in attendance. That is why you are there; you know that for some of them, your presence is more important than their parents'. For some of them, you are their parent. Thank you for the dances you have sponsored. Although you will eventually lose all hearing because we can only give our eardrums so much abuse, the students saw you dance. Thank you for attending the things the students consider important.

Thank you for your enthusiasm. You have made subjects interesting for students. They would have never appreciated what you teach except that you drove it home. In order to be successful, you had to brainstorm and come up with ways to reach students. Thank you for taking the effort to make the lessons exciting.

Thank you for making a difference in the lives of the families you touch. There are a multitude of accolades that you will never receive. You have brought families closer together because it is the nature of your heart. There are parents who are lucky their child had you because they are not in jail right now for the damage they would have inflicted on the child otherwise. You advised their child on what to say and how to react. You advised them on what their child is going through. You are making a huge difference. They were just as scared as their child going in to middle school and you have made them feel comfortable.

Thank you for the money you have spent on your classroom. Although I am sure you were thrifty with much of your décor, you have spent an untold amount of money at the end of the day, because you wanted things to be right. Students have inadvertently broken some of your furniture and you have reluctantly replaced it because you wanted them to have a great learning station. You spend money for consumables because it is absolutely impossible to remember you needed that item four months in advance for a purchase order. I am sure you have even painted on more than one occasion, using your own resources. You have spent thousands and you would do it all over again because you believe there is a cause for the money you are spending. You know it will enrich the lives of students and you count it worthy.

Thank you for the students you have mentored. They found you. They found themselves because of you. They have forever cemented you as a foundational pillar in their life. You gave them the time of day and cared what was happening in their life. Most of them have moved on and you rarely see or hear from them, but they remember you. They may not remember one amazing lesson you taught, but they remember your character. They remember the stories you told. They tell the stories you told them to their own children. Thank you for making that impact. Our society will forever be indebted, even if they don't know it.

Thank you for getting a second job to make ends meet. Of course you have every summer off and only work 185 days a year, says the parent who doesn't have a clue. There is plenty of time to get other work done, I am certain. Most positions that require a certain level of education and responsibility do not have a normal expectancy of second simultaneous careers, but you have accepted the norm and embraced the opportunity to make ends meet. You must be thrifty if you want your money to go very far.

Thank you for ignoring the negativity. Almost every book on education is about the failures. The sky is always falling. The teachers are never good enough. The money is never there. It is absolutely exhausting hearing how teachers are not meeting the needs of their students. It is also very troubling that the burden of their problems somehow lie in education. The newspapers report the bad and politicians get a whole lot of press when they complain about education. Educators are either constantly on the defense, or they begin to ignore the pundits in favor of connecting with students and creatively planning lessons to reach students. Great job for choosing the latter, you have a reward in life much greater than money, attention, or popularity.

Thank you for making a difference in the lives of students. Every day you put smiles on faces. You make the toughest age the most fun. You look past the awkwardness and smell to see that wonderful potential. There are thousands of people who know your name, but you may not remember half of them. You are making a huge difference because you answered the call to teach. None of those thousands of former students remember their test score, they remember how you made them feel. Your impact will be felt forever.

Thank you for your involvement in extra-curricular activities. The clubs you led and the community service that you provided were prime opportunities for real world learning. You might not have gotten paid, but you fielded the complaints when you cancelled, so you know they loved it. You taught students how to serve others. You made a group of the naturally most selfish individuals become selfless. You basically worked miracles every day.

Thank you for clothing the needy and feeding the hungry. You never thought you would buy some else's lunch, but it has occurred more times than you wish to explain to your spouse. You just can't watch a student go hungry, no matter how much they can get under your skin. You have given away coats, bought coats and begged for coats. You have seen dirty clothes to the point it has made you sick. You have mentioned the word deodorant for the first time to kids. They didn't teach you this in college. You cannot stand for a student to not have their essential needs met.

There are a million rewards you get by seeing the difference made in a life, but none feels as great as a thank you by those you affected. Once in a while, a student will stop by and articulate the difference that you made in their life. Most of the time, you will never understand the true impact you have made by your decision to invest in middle school and answer the call to teach.

I hope you have read this as a word of encouragement, words of affirmation that you make a difference every day that no other person can accomplish. Thank you.

THE END

References

DuFour, Richard, and Robert E. Eaker. Professional Learning Communities at Work: Best Practices for Enhancing Student Achievement. Bloomington, IN: National Education Service, 1998. Print.

Fay, Jim, and David Funk. Teaching with Love & Logic: Taking Control of the Classroom. Print.

A Few Good Men. Dir. Rob Reiner. Prod. Rob Reiner, David Brown, and Andrew Scheinman. By Aaron Sorkin. Perf. Aaron Sorkin, Tom Cruise, Jack Nicholson, Demi Moore, and Kevin Bacon. Columbia Pictures, 1992.

Jurassic Park. Dir. Steven Spielberg. By Michael Crichton and David Koepp. Perf. Sam Neill, Laura Dern, and Richard Attenborough. Universal Pictures, 1993.

Wong, Harry K., and Rosemary Tripi. Wong. The First Days of School: How to Be an Effective Teacher. Mountain View, Calif: Wong, 1998. Print.

A special thank you to the following people who have impacted me and encouraged my approach to the middle. They make the impossible possible every day.

Thank you **Meg Deweese** for being the greatest mentor teacher. I can't believe I was blessed with such an incredible teacher who forced me out of the box. You are the funniest person I have ever met. Your impact in education is immeasurable. Thank you **Tom Padalino** for your model of leadership, friendship and implementing the best practices of middle school. You have showcased your school for thousands of educators to be enriched. You have given thousands of students the greatest middle school experience. Thank you **Theresa Miller, Julie Giovannetti** and **Sonja Jenner** for your constant focus on the student above all else. You never sway from the true purpose of your call and you genuinely care about students. Thank you for serving on every committee because we were planning great things for students. We have made a great team! Thank you **Lexie Radebaugh** for giving me the opportunity to lead others. Thank you **Pam Bressler** for introducing me to special education and making me love each student individually. Thank you **Tammy Berlin** for your diligence and creativity. Thank you **Shannon McKinney** for constantly keeping me grounded. You are   amazing in every position you accept. Thank you **Lance Lutke, Cheryl Herard** and **Dave Mueller**. Thank you **Rick Johnson** for increasing the level of energy and focus toward students each year. You have reached thousands. Thank you **Marsh Boomer** for showing the students how to suck the marrow from the bones of this life. You have lived and I want to be you when I grow up. Thank you **Kyle Minton, Steve Nett** and **Deborah Ray**. Thank you **Tina Ewing** for your no nonsense approach, because anything that distracts from the students is pure nonsense. You keep people grounded. Thank you **Brie Miller** for your compassionate heart for the hurting. You haven't just increased reading abilities, you make a difference in their personal lives. Thank you **Tonya Knollmeyer, Kelsey Bridges** and **Michelle Naturale**. Thank you **Chris VanSteenvoort**. You are not just an amazing English teacher; you take care of the needs of other teachers. Every kid loves Mrs. Van. Thank you **Mike Lawson** for your intensity for learning history. I would have loved your class. Thank you **Cathye Hotaling, Terry Hughes, Andrea Jacobs** and **Donna Hogan.** Thank you **Audrey Doctor** for having faith in me to fill your shoes. It was impossible, but I found my place. Thank you **Amy McDaniel** for being my perfect teammate in the classroom. We had a blast! Thank you **Tony Ruiz** for being a great teacher buddy down the hall and keeping me grounded in my faith. Thank you **Lisa Johnson** for consistently holding down the fort at Madison. You have been the rock for so many students and staff. Thank you **Morgan Axsom** for being a great advocate and interpreter for our special education students. Thank you **Janna Griffin, Barbara Marley, Carey Dunlop** and **Maria Serrano.** Thank you **Rhonda Williams** for being the face of our school. You make us look good. Thank you **Michelle Brown** for quietly taking care of all students. Thank you **Jeanette Swygard** for constantly looking for ways to improve instruction. Thank you **Greg Carr** for your dedication to take all students and teaching them to play in the orchestra. You go above and beyond. Thank you **Christy Orphin** for your love of all students. Thank you **Terry Reynolds** for making sure all students can be physically successful. Thank you **Alex Rivera** for passionately accepting all students just as they are and expecting to hear a sweet sound from each one. Thank you **Sarah Stevens, Wendy Benford,** and **Casey Brewer.** Thank you **Brent Massey** for bringing excitement and character to class every day. Thank you **Keri Bostwick** for meticulously editing the entire book and encouraging me. You have a gift to encourage others. Thank you **Bev Smith**, you are amazing at adapting to the needs of others. Thank you **Deb French** for leaving the littles and joining the middle. You bring such a great humor to every situation. Thank you **Renee Arnold, Joanna Childress,** and **Rachel Hough.** Thank you **Patty Strothman** for the rigor and expectation you brought to the classroom. Students had to step up to meet your expectations. Thank you **Mark Villines** for calmly approaching such an intense position and recruiting a magnificent band. Thank you **Mildred German, Sophia Sayles** and **Tiffany Munn**. Thank you **Lisa Burton** for choosing to teach as a second career. You inspire others every day. Thank you **Kyle Ppool** for settling down at Madison. You bring life to class and energy to school every day. Thank you **Liz Martin, Marsha Weddington, Angel Smith,** and **Joey Newsome**. Thank you **Andy Thurman** for connecting to those whom nobody else can. Thank you **John Hammack** for your work ethic. You are a rock. Thank you **Sasha Yorman** for being an amazing English teacher. It is your call. Thank you **Tina Gray** and **Kari Davis** for teaching others to love those that are different. Thank you **Julie Brown** for bringing your skills to our counseling department. Thank you **Holly Martin** for bringing your kindness and calmness to our counseling department. Thank you **Esther Shigley** for the amazing impact you had on everyone you touched. Thank you **Andrew Blain, Tony Villalobos,** and **Laura Williams**. Thank you **Chuck McCauley** for your discernment and leadership. Thank you **Courtney Fuller** for your fresh ideas and commitments to make them successful. Thank you **Jennifer Cubbage** for always making it work. Thank you **Matt Hancock** for sharpening our beliefs in education and life. Thank you **Tiffany Palmer, Linda Bradford** and **Melanie Jay**. Thank you **Kerry Combs** for showing that a rookie teacher can be amazing beyond her experience. Thank you **Steve Hughes** for showing that an experienced and knowledgeable professor can still learn from middle school students. Thank you **Lori Shelley** for quietly making math the most exciting class. Thank you **Ryan Huff, Keri Gardner, Sam Herriman, Bud Sexson, Janet Vernon, Dr. Quinn** and **Greg Tackett**. Thank you **TJ Mears** (or **JT Myers**) for your passion to reach students. It has connected us for two decades.

Thank you Amanda, Anna and Fletcher.

CPSIA information can be obtained
at www.ICGtesting.com
Printed in the USA
FFOW05n0602070617
36468FF

9 780997 552010